INSIDE
FIGURE SKATING

INSIDE
Figure Skating

ALINA SIVORINOVSKY

MetroBooks

MetroBooks

An Imprint of Friedman/Fairfax Publishers

Author's note: The text for this book was prepared prior to the developments of the 1998–99 season.

Library of Congress Cataloging-in-Publication Data
Sivorinosky, Alina
    Inside figure skating / Alina Sivorinosky.
        p.   cm.
    Includes index.
    ISBN 1-56799-777-5
    1. Skating. 2. Skating—History. I.title.
GV850.4.S52 1999
796.91'2—dc21   99-30242
                                                    CIP

ISBN 1-56799-777-5

Editor: Ann Kirby
Art Director: Jeff Batzli
Designer: Christina Grupico
Photography Editor: Valerie E. Kennedy
Production Manager: Richela Fabian

Color separations by Spectrum Pte. Ltd.
Printed and bound in Great Britain by Butler & Tanner Ltd, Frome and London

10 9 8 7 6 5 4 3 2 1

For bulk purchases and special sales, please contact:

Friedman/Fairfax Publishers
Attention: Sales Department
15 West 26th Street
New York, NY 10010
212/685-6610 FAX 212/685-1307

Visit our website:
http://www.metrobooks.com

24.95

ACKNOWLEDGMENTS

A heartfelt thank-you to all the people
who have made my various skating projects
so enjoyable over the years:

Judy Blumberg
Brian Boitano
Christopher Bowman
Dick Button
Chris Carmody
Peter Carruthers
Alice Cook
Kathy Cook
Robin Cousins
Lois Elfman
Peggy Fleming
Terry Gannon
Norman Grossfeld
Jean Hall
Brian Klavano
Cindy Lang
Ralph Mole
Kristen Moore
Sandra Neil
Larry Nuekum
Carol Probst
Jirina Ribbens
Lana Sherman
Mark Smith
Kellie Snyder
Rosalyn Sumners
Gorsha Sur
Tiffany Trigg
Bob Varsha
Lesley Visser
Geri Walbert
Doug Wilson

...with an extra-special thanks to Meg Streeter

END OF THE INNOCENCE

ALTHOUGH THE LADIES' FINALS AT BOTH KATARINA WITT'S (ABOVE) AND KRISTI YAMAGUCHI'S (OPPOSITE) OLYMPICS WERE THE HIGHEST-RATED SHOWS OF THEIR RESPECTIVE GAMES, NEITHER COULD MEASURE UP TO THE RECORD-BREAKING SKATING EXPLOSION OF 1994.

O nce, the line between amateur and professional skaters was drawn as solidly as a figure eight etched into the ice. Professional skaters could earn money for skating. Amateur skaters could not.

Amateur skaters blearily stumbled out of bed before the crack of dawn and spent hour after hour inside foggy, frigid ice rinks, blowing puffs of warm air onto their freezing hands and going through boxes of tissues for their runny noses. They practiced figures and jumps and spins and lifts and dances, all in the hopes of winning at the upcoming National, World, and Olympic Championships—and with enough medals, they would someday warrant an invitation to join a professional ice show or performance company.

They would then trade in their 5 A.M. wake-up calls for late nights in rambling buses and crowded airports, a whirling succession of hotel rooms, a grueling schedule of twenty-eight cities in thirty days—and the deep satisfaction of making a living doing what they loved most, in the company of people who shared their passion. Turning pro also meant the chance to skate in professional competitions where a first, second, third, and even fourth place medal brought not only glory, but financial compensation.

Once, a skater needed to choose which of those two lives he or she wanted—amateur or professional. Nobody could do both at the same time. As soon as the door permanently closed on the former—when a skater accepted money for performing or competing or coaching or appearing in a commercial—he or she stayed the latter forever. There was no going back.

All that changed in 1994, when professional skaters from all over the world were allowed to "reinstate" and compete, once again, at their Nationals and at the Olympics.

The 1994 Olympics also marked the beginning of a new popularity for skating, and the fan base worldwide grew exponentially. Suddenly, skating was hot, and both competitions and exhibitions mulitplied. Where there had once been, at most, four professional competitions to attend in a year, now there were twenty—and the number kept growing. Where there had once been an exhibition or two to give a year, now there were one or two a month, then one or two a week.

With so many new competitions and tours to fill, the chance to participate was no longer limited to just the major names on the pro circuit—Olympic gold medalists like Katarina Witt, Brian Boitano, Kristi Yamaguchi, or Torvill and Dean. Lesser-known pros like 1984 Olympic silver medalist Rosalynn Sumners, 1984 Olympic bronze medalist Jozef Sabovcik, and 1987 world bronze medalist Caryn Kadavy—and even some skaters with no major world titles whatsoever like Lisa-Marie Allen, Scott Williams, and Renee Roca and Gorsha Sur—were welcomed into the shows.

Meanwhile, "amateur" skaters, who were still paying for lessons, costumes, and travel were forbidden to earn anything for their efforts. Their performances at big-draw competitions like the

Olympics, the World Championship, and the U.S. Championship were drawing Super Bowl–level ratings and important revenue for the television networks, the federations that sold their broadcast rights, and the event sponsors. The only ones not deriving income from the newly popular sport were the amateur skaters who had brought it to the public's attention in the first place.

Is it any wonder, then, that the International Skating Union (ISU), concerned at the prospect of losing its popular amateurs to the rewards of professional skating, buckled under and announced that, come 1995, the newly dubbed "eligible" skaters, like their also renamed "ineligible" counterparts, would no longer be penalized for making a living from what they excelled at? In fact, without risking

WHEN FRENCH NATIONAL CHAMPION PHILIPPE CANDELORO PERFORMED AT THE 1994 OLYMPICS, OVER 50 PERCENT OF HIS COUNTRY TUNED IN TO WATCH. AS A RESULT, THE FRENCH FEDERATION WAS ABLE TO SELL SUBSEQUENT SKATING TELEVISION RIGHTS TO TF1 FOR $2.8 MILLION DOLLARS. THE HEAVILY INVESTED TELEVISION CHANNEL THEN PERSUADED THE FEDERATION TO PUT PRESSURE ON ITS STAR TO REMAIN ELIGIBLE FOR THE 1998 OLYMPICS.

Maria Butyrskaya, 1999 World champion, chose to remain eligible after finishing fourth at the 1998 Olympics. In her mind, there was no longer a difference between professional and amateur skating.

their Olympic-eligible status, those skaters who abided by ISU rules and competed only in ISU-sanctioned competitions would be able to earn prize money for participating in a newly created Champions' Series of five internationals as well as for taking part in Pro/Ams, with eligible and ineligible skaters going head-to-head in a team format, the World Championship, and even the 1998 Olympics. These skaters could also be paid for appearing in made-for-television events like *Too Hot to Skate*, *Skating Romance*, *The Art of Russian Skating*, and *Skates of Gold* or for starring in their own tour.

Carol Heiss Jenkins, a 1960 Olympic champion, believes that there is an upside to the rule change in that "parents don't have to put a second mortgage on their home to pay for a child's skating." But there is also a downside: "The family expects [their skater] to earn a certain amount. We used to hear, 'Wouldn't it be wonderful to be the best?' Now, the money is all."

According to ISU president Ottavio Cinquanta, "[Now] eligible skaters are more professional, if you mean professional is working hard and making skating your profession."

Thanks to skating's increased exposure on television and its subsequent popularity, eligible skaters ranging from American world champions Michelle Kwan, Todd Eldredge, and Tara Lipinski to former Soviets like Ilia Kulik, Irina Slutskaya, and Maria Butyrskaya to French superstars Surya Bonaly and Philippe Candeloro stepped into an unprecedented "best of both worlds" era.

In 1995, when the only difference left between eligible and ineligible skaters proved to be who they wanted to accept money from—the ISU (which left you eligible for Olympic competition) or an unsanctioned promoter (which left you ineligible)—every capable skater in the world became a salaried professional.

Lights, Camera, Axel: How Television Changed Skating

I n June 1996, *Skating* magazine, the official publication of the 125,000-member United States Figure Skating Association (USFSA), asked its readers to vote on which development had the greatest impact on figure skating in the U.S. in the past seventy-five years. In last place came the Harding/Kerrigan incident of 1994, often cited by those outside the sport as the turning point in skating's transformation from a once-every-four-years novelty to the second most watched athletic endeavor (after football) in America.

Nancy Kerrigan, a 1994 Olympic silver medalist, resents such talk, taking offense at the idea that a person being hurt is judged by some as "the best thing that ever happened to skating."

And the readers of *Skating* magazine agree with her. When asked to name the recent development with the greatest impact on skating, nearly 40 percent chose television.

THE TELEVISION REVOLUTION

"Nothing significant happened in the evolution of figure skating that was not influenced by television," says ABC-TV director Doug Wilson. "Television showed not only that skating was a sport that had extraordinary requirements, but that it was star-oriented, [with] dedicated, terrific, interesting people. Because in order to be very good in figure skating, you have to be an extraordinary person. The moment a skater steps on the ice, their best friend is TV. We're there to enhance what the skater is trying to say."

For Wilson, that vital process of enhancement is rooted in a strategy he first conceived while watching 1968 Olympic champion Peggy Fleming draw a diagram of her Olympic program. She was planning to send it as a Christmas card. Wilson realized he could employ a similar diagram to plan his coverage

IN 1998, AS ALL FIGURE-SKATING EYES TURNED TO THE WINTER OLYMPICS, 1968 CHAMPION PEGGY FLEMING REVEALED SHE WAS BATTLING BREAST CANCER. AS A RESULT, SHE WAS UNABLE TO ASSUME HER REGULAR PLACE AS COMMENTATOR FOR THE WORLD CHAMPIONSHIPS A MONTH LATER.

of each skater's routine in advance. He began inviting skaters to draw him their programs as their music played, and made notes on the timing of their elements. Unfortunately, Wilson found out that what he often ended up with was a stack of scribbles. When he was directing Pro Skate in 1983, a lack of time to sit with every skater and review his or her program compelled him to ask his assistant to monitor the clock and take notes while Wilson watched the rehearsal and called out his camera cues on the fly. This improvisation developed into the two-person system that Wilson and every other skating director use today.

For him, it's a labor of love. His motto is, "The moment a director is about to display to the person in their living room a triple axel that Todd Eldredge has rehearsed forty thousand times for that moment—then, by God, that's worth attention, it's worth caring, and the value of that better be respected."

But television doesn't merely observe and record skating. As asserted by the readers of *Skating* magazine, television's presence has actually caused a series of revolutions in the sport.

One significant TV-inspired reorganization took place in the early 1970s, thanks to five-time U.S. ladies' champion Janet Lynn. (Lynn had triggered a much smaller effect when her comment at the 1968 Olympics—that what she missed most about home was McDonald's hamburgers—inspired the company to send enough burgers for every U.S. athlete and, eight years later, become the Games' sponsor.)

In 1972, when Lynn competed at her second Olympics, compulsory figures counted for 60 percent of a skater's score, the free-skating for 40 percent. Lynn was a brilliant jumper and spinner, but a mediocre tracer of figures. Her closest competitor, 1972 Olympic champion Beatrix "Trixie" Schuba of Austria, was a lethargic freestyler but arguably the greatest figure skater the world had ever seen. By the time the televised portion of the event, the free-skating, rolled around, Trixie was usually so far ahead that all she had to do was remain alive to

capture the title. Viewers at home, however, could not understand why Trixie was the winner when Lynn had skated so enchantingly only moments earlier. As a result, following the 1972 Olympics, a short program, worth 20 percent of the score, was added to all skating contests and the value of figures was reduced, making a final tally of figures 30 percent, freestyle (combined short and long programs) 70 percent. Over the next eighteen years, as skating grew in popularity, television viewers complained that figures were dull. So in 1990, the figures were tossed altogether.

Meg Streeter, who directs skating for Fox, ABC, USA, A&E, UPN, and Turner and still mourns the loss of compulsory figures, does believe that their elimination provided one benefit: "The elimination of figures [made] judging get better. In the old days, if judges wanted someone in particular to win, since figures were the first event out, they could inflate their scores, and *the audience would never see it.* Because the audience wasn't watching, things could happen that nobody knew about. But by televising an event you have more feedback as to how the judging goes. When you have a decision that people complain about around the world, it's going to have an impact. Now, judging has improved a great deal. It's more reflective of what's really happening."

Concurs Wilson, "Skating changed because of the size of the audience witnessing it." By pointing its inquisitive eye onto the sport, television not only increased skating's popularity, it changed the very nature and rules of the game. Figures were just the tip of the iceberg.

For years, whenever producers of ABC's *Wide World of Sports* were asked by an eager athlete, "How do I get on TV?" the standard response was always, "Either win or be spectacular." At the 1972 Worlds, an up-and-coming American skater fulfilled the second condition. Wilson remembers that he was so smitten by a girl with a big pink bow that he broke precedent and, in the middle of the dance event, "flashed back" to show a ladies' competitor who hadn't won a medal. He had given the world its first glimpse of a teenage Dorothy Hamill.

Skating and television broke another precedent in 1980 when a group of amateur and pro skaters, including Peggy Fleming, Lisa-Marie Allen, Linda Fratianne, JoJo Starbuck and Kenneth Shelley, Tai Babilonia and Randy Gardner, Judy Blumberg and Michael Seibert, David Santee, and Elaine Zayak—skaters who, under the old amateur and pro rules, should not have been performing on the same ice—became the first U.S. skaters to perform in Communist China. Apparently, one of Peggy Fleming's television specials had aired there, raising interest in her performing live and opening a door to the historic visit. The U.S. ambassador later told the athletes that what they had done to promote goodwill between the U.S. and China was worth a thousand political speeches.

The 1980 show aired live in China and was seen by 200 million people. Among them may have been a three-year-old Chen Lu, who, after winning the 1995 World Championship, disclosed that her childhood idol had been Peggy Fleming.

But in recent years, skating has reached a level of popularity that just ten years ago would have been unfathomable. The public's increased interest in the sport—fueled in part by headline-grabbing competitions and controversies made televised competitions quite profitable for the networks. And as coverage increased, skating's audience increased as well.

In 1994, CBS had just lost its coverage of the National Football League. That same year, USFSA president Claire Ferguson and executive director Jerry Lace wrote, "This glut of skating stems from...CBS scrambling to fill [a] void. Skating became a favorite filler because of the potential

ratings." Jirina Ribbens, Vice-President of Candid Productions, which produces the World Professional Championships, agrees. "The boys in sports would have never thought of skating if it hadn't gotten such high ratings at the Olympics, and it was cheap, comparatively speaking."

What made figure skating so cheap for CBS to acquire was that the sports-promotion company Jefferson Pilot, which owned quite a few affiliate stations, began buying time for made-for-TV programs like *Ice Wars* and *Too Hot to Skate*. (The company first went into the skating business in 1991 because Katarina Witt was then one of their clients and they wanted a venue in which to showcase her.) In 1996, despite executive Mike Burg's vow that they wouldn't create an event "just for the sake of doing it," six new skating shows soon popped up on the small screen.

Streeter is quick to add that it wasn't just CBS that increased their skating coverage: "It was all the networks. When UPN decided to put on their first live broadcast ever, it was a skating event, the U.S. Open. The USA network now has three or four skating shows on. Turner has a quota of skating shows they want to get on the air. So it's not just CBS putting on skating to replace football. ABC added the Pro/Ams, and extended their contract for Nationals and Worlds." NBC broadcast the World Professional Championship, and in 1997, Fox had most of the Champions' Series and its final. ABC picked it up for the 1999–2000 season.

Stresses Streeter, "Every network and all the cable networks have gone out of their way to seek out skating shows."

WORKING WITH THE MEDIA

As skaters grew more accustomed to having television cameras recording their every step, they also grew accustomed to making the concessions necessary to ensure that the cameras captured everything

IN APRIL OF 1989, WORLD PAIR CHAMPION TAI BABILONIA TOLD HER STORY OF DRUG ABUSE, DEPRESSION, AND SUICIDE ATTEMPTS TO PEOPLE MAGAZINE. A WEEK LATER, HER MANAGER CLOSED A DEAL WITH NBC FOR A BIOGRAPHICAL TELEVISION MOVIE. ON THIN ICE: THE TAI BABILONIA STORY AIRED IN NOVEMBER OF 1990.

they needed to make the skater look good. At the 1980 Olympics, when a production assistant overslept and missed a mandatory shot of Linda Fratianne arriving for practice, the four-time U.S. champion graciously agreed to reenact the moment for the cameras.

By 1984, Scott Hamilton was so television-savvy that he called up ABC and said, "I don't know if you're going to do an up-close-and-personal profile on me, but I suspect it's possible. I thought of this piece of music sung by Gary Morris, 'Wind Beneath My Wings,' and it's everything I believe about my relationship with my coach, Don Laws. So, if you were going to do a piece on me, I just want to throw

that in." Laughs ABC-TV's Doug Wilson, "He was already producing!"

At the 1988 Olympics, there was a plan was to make Russian pair skater Ekaterina Gordeeva the media darling of the show. It was a fine plan but it could have been hampered by the fact that pairs was, and typically still is, the first discipline to finish competition. This meant that an immense buildup was impossible. Undaunted, the television producers refused to abstain from their original scheme, so even though she'd already won the gold, Gordeeva stayed on the air for the entire duration of the Games, whether she was walking around the Athletes' Village or simply sitting in the stands.

ABC'S UP-CLOSE-AND-PERSONAL COVERAGE OF THE 1988 OLYMPICS INTRODUCED AMERICA TO THE ULTRA-EXPRESSIVE FACES OF EKATERINA GORDEEVA (WITH HER LATE PARTNER, SERGEI GRINKOV, OPPOSITE) AND BRIAN BOITANO (LEFT). DESPITE THE EMERGENCE OF THREE MORE GENERATIONS (1992, 1994, 1998) OF OLYMPIC CHAMPIONS, BOTH GORDEEVA AND BOITANO REMAIN TWO OF THE MOST POPULAR PROFESSIONALS ON THE CIRCUIT.

going so far as to pop in on an editing session and ask the producer in charge to climb out of her chair so that Katarina might sit in it and look like she was the one supervising the show. The producer politely declined.

By 1994, French champion Philippe Candeloro took collaboration with the media a significant step further. When a CBS producer pointed out that a moment of his program would be more effective if focused at a particular camera, Philippe actually took the advice and changed his presentation—and won the bronze medal.

At eligible competitions, television producers claim that they try their best to be unobtrusive and not disturb the natural rhythm of the sport. Yet at a live event, a production assistant is often stationed by the judges' desk to ensure that marks are revealed at *television's* convenience. A nervous skater may be sitting in the kiss-and-cry area, waiting to see results that will affect the rest of his or her life, but if there happens to be a commercial at the moment, the skater will just have to wait a tad longer.

On the other hand, television producers don't mind getting involved with professional competitions, operating on the philosophy that the skaters and producers are working together to present the best show possible. For instance, at the 1995 Challenge of Champions, Wilson said, "Yuka Sato [the 1994 world champion from Japan] had a moment of presentation which was on one side of the arena, between what would be the blue [hockey] line and the red line. I presumptuously asked if she thought she might be able to rechoreograph that a

Another idea that didn't come off quite as planned was Wilson's coverage of Brian Boitano's long program. Wilson was determined to catch the definitive head-turn at the onset of the routine, in all its Napoleonic glory. But as it turned out, "I'd planned an opening shot, a first shot of his face, before the head-turn, but because something happened prior to his going out on the ice, the camera I'd planned to use was not available. I had to use another one, in the left corner. It turned out to be a better shot than what I planned. Which, again, proves that if you really work hard and do your homework, it's amazing how lucky you can get."

In 1992, 1984 and 1988 Olympic champion Katarina Witt showed how much she'd learned about the positive PR power of media images. While working as a backstage reporter for CBS, Witt invited a German camera crew to film her in action. She gave them a tour of the CBS complex, boasting about her assorted roles in the production, even

ALTHOUGH IT CAN BE DIFFICULT TO MAINTAIN A PERSONAL LIFE WHILE TOURING AND COMPETING, TWO-TIME OLYMPIC BRONZE MEDALIST PHILIPPE CANDELORO (RIGHT) WED HIS GIRLFRIEND OF SIX YEARS, OLIVIA DARMON, IN SEPTEMBER OF 1998, WHILE WORLD CHAMPION YUKA SATO (OPPOSITE), THE SAME YEAR, ANNOUNCED HER ENGAGEMENT TO FELLOW SKATER JASON DUNGJEN. WHEN DUNGJEN AND PAIR PARTNER KYOKO INA BROKE UP, SATO ALSO TOOK UP PAIR SKATING WITH HER HUSBAND-TO-BE.

COACH FRANK
CARROLL HAD HIS
HEART BROKEN FOR
THE SECOND TIME IN
HIS CAREER, WHEN
STAR PUPIL
MICHELLE KWAN
FAILED TO WIN GOLD
AT THE 1998
OLYMPICS. EIGHTEEN
YEARS EARLIER, IN
LAKE PLACID,
CARROLL'S PRO-
TEGÉE, DEFENDING
WORLD CHAMPION
LINDA FRATIANNE,
ALSO CAME IN SEC-
OND. IN 1980,
CARROLL ACCUSED
THE JUDGES OF
NATIONALISTIC BIAS
FOR PUTTING AN
EAST GERMAN GIRL
AHEAD OF AN
AMERICAN.

little, so when she stopped to make that presentation, she was at the red line position, in front of my camera. Skaters want to make eye contact with the audience...[but for television, that means] they're looking away. What they want to do to the audience of one thousand people in front of them, they're not doing to the TV audience that's 10 million. If they're about to present themselves to the world, it's better if we see their faces."

However, sometimes the face television presents to the world is not necessarily the one the skater wants. Wilson asks, "How long, especially if you're live, are skaters sitting in kiss-and-cry and you're looking at their eyes and you're looking at their tears and you're looking at their emotions and you get to see what kind of people they are? You can see if they have grace under pressure, or if they're not as admirable."

THE GOOD, THE BAD, AND THE CONTROVERSIAL

Those less admirable attributes brought up by the media and grumbled about by the skaters include 1994 Olympic silver medalist Nancy Kerrigan's less than kind remarks about rival Oksana Baiul (and about Mickey Mouse); Baiul's 1997 drunk-driving charges; 1995 U.S. champion Nicole Bobek's arrest for felony burglary; Canadian medalist Gary Beacom's jail term for failure to pay taxes; French champion Surya Bonaly's romantic claims of being born on Reunion Island, despite being born in Nice; and U.S. ice dance champions Punsalan and Swallow's petition to keep their main opponent, Russian-born Gorsha Sur, of Roca and Sur, from getting his American citizenship in time to challenge them for the United States' only 1994 Olympic

berth. Punsalan and Swallow freely admitted their deed on television and then, stunned by the backlash their confession produced, blamed ABC for airing the segment and refused to grant the network any interviews for more than a year.

On the other hand, skaters are not averse to using the press if it promotes their agenda. In 1997, when Russian world and Olympic dance champions Grishuk and Platov split with their coach, 1980 Olympic champion Natalia Linichuk, they chose to fight all their battles exclusively in the press. In December 1996, Grishuk and Platov, having been off the ice for a majority of the season due to Platov's knee injury, allegedly traveled home to Moscow for a secret meeting with the Russian Skating Federation. There they sought a guarantee that they would win all the competitions they entered leading up to the 1998 Olympics. The members of the federation told them that they could provide no such guarantee. Grishuk and Platov then returned to their home base in Newark, Delaware, to ask Linichuk (who also coached 1996 world silver medalists Krylova and Ovsianikov) to ensure another year of victory for them by deliberately weakening the second team. When Linichuk refused, Grishuk and Platov split for Marlboro,

Massachusetts, and Tatiana Tarasova, trainer of 1996 world silver medalist Ilia Kulik. At the 1997 European Championship, after Grishuk and Platov's new dances won them not only the gold but an almost record-breaking twelve perfect 6.0s (England's Torvill and Dean still hold the record of seventeen 6.0s at the 1984 Europeans), Linichuk tried to take credit for the stunning victory by claiming she'd participated in choreographing their new numbers. Grishuk categorically denied the contention, adding, "Let God be her judge."

God, or at least the Russian media, who sided squarely with the skaters over their ex-coach, asserted in 6.0, the official publication of the Russian Skating Federation, "Linichuk did everything in her power to push Grishuk and Platov into the professional realm. This duo had already done their thing for her [won Olympic gold] and she was convinced it was time for them to leave." At the subsequent Worlds, the Ukrainian media got into the act, ruminating about their national champions, Romanova and Yaroshenko, who also trained under Linichuk: "One can only feel sorry for the athletes. Their mentor will never make champions of them. Linichuk always places her bets on the Russian athletes. As long as [Romanova and Yaroshenko] keep training with Linichuk, they will see medals hang only on the necks of their opponents."

Within months of the media declaring Natalia Linichuk persona non grata in skating circles, the coach, who at the 1996 Europeans saw a podium filled with only her skaters (Grishuk and Platov, gold; Krylova and Ovsianikov, silver; Romanova and Yaroshenko, bronze), was down to one winning team. Heeding the advice of the Ukrainian press, Romanova and Yaroshenko also defected to Tarasova, chalking up another example of media coverage that didn't just observe, but affected events.

Of course, there are those who claim that controversy is good for skating. After all, despite what readers of *Skating* magazine might think, didn't the Tonya Harding/Nancy Kerrigan saga trigger the current boom of interest in the sport?

Streeter believes that it wasn't the incident itself that drew viewers, so much as the fact that television covered it: "If a TV camera had not been there to see Nancy's reaction—it made very powerful television which people will remember for a long time—if we had only heard about the attack and never seen it, I don't think it ever would have been quite the event it became. [Nancy] sitting on the ground, saying 'Why, me?' made people want to stop, look, listen, and then want to follow [the story]. In following it, they then got hooked on skating.

People who'd never watched skating began watching. The nice thing is they stayed with it over the course of the next four years. Ironically, skating benefited from a criminal act. Had television not been there to bring it to people, we would not have had the increased viewership."

But that increased viewership did not, as many conjectured, lead to the increase of skating coverage that erupted on television almost immediately afterward. Jirina Ribbens, vice president of Candid Productions, which produced the World Professional Championship, contends, "The popularity of skating at the 1994 Games made it interesting for TV, but it's not what caused the boom. What caused the boom was extra programming." With increased coverage of skating, on CBS in particular, a public turned on by the Kerrigan/Harding incident tuned in to televised competition.

TELEVISION AND THE 1998 OLYMPICS

Eager to surpass even the figure skating frenzy of 1994, American coverage of the 1998 Winter Olympics in Nagano, Japan, didn't limit itself merely to CBS-TV's televising the competition bracketed by tear-jerking or uplifting personality features on either side. TNT also got into the act, trying to attract the soap-opera and talk-show audiences with a daily afternoon talk show of their own, *The Cutting Edge*, devoted exclusively to figure skating. Peter Carruthers and Rosalynn Sumners, both 1984 Olympic silver medalists, and 1976 Olympian Alice Cook hosted the show from a set erected in the corner of the practice rink, where any spill a skater took in practice could now be instantly pointed out and dissected. Since CBS held first broadcast rights to the actual competition, *The Cutting Edge* made do with rink-note gossip, predictions, speculations, and playing "fashion police" for some of the more atrocious costume choices.

Along with the two American networks and a host of local TV and radio stations, the athletes found themselves being covered and commented on by announcers from Canada, France, Germany, Australia, Russia, Great Britain, Poland, Ukraine, China, and both NHK and TBS of Japan. Many broadcast teams were anchored by former competitive skaters, several of whom now worked as choreographers or coaches for the same skaters whose performances they were commenting on.

As analyst for Canada's CBC, 1984 world pair champion Paul Martini was forbidden from even giving the appearance of coaching his team, 1997 Canadian champions Marie-Claude Savard-Gagnon and Luc Bradet. As a result, he had to sit and watch helplessly as, during the long program, his

Robin Cousins, 1980 Olympic champion and choreographer for 1998 U.S. bronze medalist Nicole Bobek, found himself in the same boat in 1998, while he was providing commentary for the BBC. By the time Nicole finished stumbling and tripping through short and long programs that mired her in a record-low seventeenth place, Cousins was asserting on the air that barely three steps of his original work had made it to the competition.

Lea Ann Miller, 1984 U.S. pair silver medalist, had things a little easier. As an associate producer for CBS-TV, she did not have to be on camera feigning objectivity while her student, Japan's own teen sensation Takeshi Honda, skated his programs. Working only off-camera, Miller was free to take off her headset and nervously burrow her fingers into the arm of a CBS analyst, 1988 Olympic bronze dance medalist Tracy Wilson.

flu-stricken skaters nearly collasped. Dizzy and sick, Savard-Gagnon and Bradet were obliged to interrupt their routine in order to shakily compose themselves.

Sitting by Martini in the CBC booth was five-time Canadian pair champion Sandra Bezic. In 1988, she had choreographed Brian Boitano's Olympic gold medal "Napoleon" program. Back then, she'd been only a spectator, visibly jumping up and down and applauding in the background as Brian completed his routine. Ten years later, as two of her newest protégées, America's Tara Lipinski and China's Lu Chen, skated to gold and bronze, respectively, Bezic was faced with presenting commentary on programs of her own design.

CONTROVERSY AT NAGANO

With the world watching every move they made, the skaters in Nagano couldn't help playing to the cameras and battling for placings not only on the ice, but among the press.

The ice dancers proved the most pugnacious. Already, television coverage of the Champions' Series, during which 1994 Olympic champs Grishuk and Platov took several falls yet continued a twenty-one-competition winning streak, had prompted so much outrage from viewers that the ISU gave in and issued the so-called Platov Rule, which mandated that, for the first time, spills would require the judges to take a mandatory score deduction. Even though he'd had a rule named

DESPITE BECOMING
THE ONLY TEAM EVER
TO WIN TWO OLYMPIC
GOLD MEDALS, PASHA
GRISHUK AND
EVGENY PLATOV
(LEFT) DISSOLVED
THEIR PARTNERSHIP
IN 1998. PLATOV
WENT ON TO SKATE
WITH 1993 WORLD
CHAMPION MAIA
USOVA, WHILE
GRISHUK TEAMED UP
WITH MAIA'S EX-HUS-
BAND, AND PASHA'S
FORMER BOYFRIEND,
SASHA ZHULIN. THE
TWO TEAMS WENT
HEAD TO HEAD FOR
THE FIRST TIME IN
COMPETITION LATER
THAT SAME YEAR. THE
TEAM OF USOVA AND
PLATOV CAME OUT
ON TOP.

LIGHTS, CAMERA, AXEL: HOW TELEVISION CHANGED SKATING

31

after him, when it came to publicity, Platov was forced to take a back seat to his controversy-loving partner, Oksana (or rather *Pasha*) Grishuk. Claiming she was tired of being confused with fellow Olympic gold medalist Oksana Baiul, Grishuk legally changed her first name to Pasha. Then, for reasons she had trouble articulating, she dyed her hair the same shade of platinum blonde as her former namesake.

Grishuk and Platov may have been in Nagano trying to become the first ice dancers ever to win two Olympic golds, but Pasha made it clear that her true goal in life was to be an American movie star. She confidently told reporters that she expected to win an Oscar in four years, and she whispered to an American television producer, "All the press wants only to talk to me." When asked where that left him,

a resigned Platov joked, "I will hit the gym, bulk up, and become her bodyguard."

Delighted with such a colorful character to track, the media enthusiastically monitored Grishuk's every move, prompting *The Cutting Edge*'s Alice Cook to observe that these Games had become all about "Pasha, Pasha, Pasha." Playing up her idolization of Marilyn Monroe, CBS even went so far as to dress Pasha up and have her sing a breathy version of "Happy Birthday, Mr. President."

Feeling that no matter what they did on ice, they'd already lost the PR battle, the other dance teams hoping to challenge for gold took time out to elaborate their own media images. Two-time world silver medalists Anjelika Krylova and Oleg Ovsianikov of Russia did their best to refocus the cameras on themselves by dressing the exquisite

Krylova in the tightest, most revealing, sexiest out-fits imaginable (even in practice). Yet even Krylova's sensational costumes couldn't distract the press for long. During a compulsory dance practice session, as soon as Krylova and Ovsianikov started their tango, Grishuk and Platov magically materialized barely a foot behind them. For sixty taut, volatile seconds, the two teams skated the same dance on the same pattern: graceful, aggressive mirror images locked in mortal combat, simultaneously trying to outdo each other and pretend they didn't know the other existed. It was the Last Tango in Nagano. It was, in the words of one producer, "orgasmic."

It was more than 1996 and 1997 world bronze medalists Shae-Lynn Bourne and Victor Kraatz of Canada could stomach. The six-time national champions came to Japan determined to become the first non-Russians since Great Britain's Torvill and Dean to win Olympic gold in ice dance, and they wasted no time launching their offensive in the media. They began by charging that Krylova and Ovsianikov were trying to intimidate them, claiming that at the Champions' Series final the Russians shoved the Canadians against the boards and then fired a series of high kicks inches from Bourne's face (at the 1998 Europeans, Krylova twice blindsided Grishuk and Platov, cutting Grishuk's arm and bruising Platov's calf). Then, after the competition began and the Canadians found themselves tied for fourth place after two compulsory dances, their coach, Natalia Dubova

(ironically herself a Russian), accused the judges of an anti-Canadian conspiracy. After the compulsories, Russians Grishuk and Platov sat in first place, with Krylova and Ovsianikov in second and the French team of Russian-born Marina Anissina and Gwendal Peizerat in third.

The media ran with the allegation, solemnly reporting over and over again that the Canadians were robbed until even those who had not seen the competition were repeating it. Then, miraculously in the world of ice dancing, where any sort of movement in placings is considered a historical achievement, by the next phase of the event the Canadians had moved up to a solid lock on fourth, followed by

OPPOSITE:
CANADIAN ICE-DANCERS SHAE-LYNN BOURNE AND VICTOR KRAATZ ALMOST FAILED TO MAKE THEIR COMPETITIVE DEBUT FOR THE 1998–1999 SEASON, WHEN THE PAIR REFUSED TO SIGN A CANADIAN FIGURE SKATING ASSOCI-ATION AGREEMENT GRANTING THE FEDERATION USE OF THEIR PHOTOGRAPHIC AND VIDEO IMAGES, FREE OF CHARGE. ONCE THE LANGUAGE WAS REWORKED TO THEIR SATISFACTION, BOURNE AND KRAATZ WENT ON TO WIN GOLD AT SKATE CANADA '98.

LEFT:
AFTER YEARS OF SWEARING THAT THEY WOULD NEVER ABANDON THEIR MOTHERLAND, RUSSIAN WORLD PAIR CHAMPIONS ELENA BEREZNAIA (LEFT) AND ANTON SIKHARULIDZE QUIETLY SPENT THE SUMMER OF 1998 TRAINING IN STAMFORD, CONNECTICUT, BEFORE ANNOUNCING THAT THEY WOULD BE RELOCATING TO THE UNITED STATES FULL TIME.

third in the final free dance—though it wasn't enough to move them into medal position.

Seeing that his skaters were almost bounced out of the bronze medal by a PR campaign, the president of the French Skating Federation asserted that it was bad form for a coach to try and change judges' opinions in the middle of a competition: "It's not fair to the judges or the skaters. Let the judges judge and let the skaters skate." But the unspoken theme of the Olympics seemed to be: let the coaches play the press.

Like Dubova, Tamara Moskvina, coach of the Russians Oksana Kazakova and Artur Dmitriev (the eventual pair champs) and of countrymen Elena Bereznaia and Anton Sikharulidze (the silver medalists), made no move unless first surrounded by the traveling cluster of reporters that one observer dubbed "Tamara's swarm." Even before the Games began, the savviest public relations player in Russia opened her home and rink to any television crews interested in shooting a profile on either of her top couples. Alloting her enthusiam equally between the two pairs, Moskvina, she retold their respective dramatic stories. When Sikharulidze complained about having to perform for the cameras, his coach reminded him curtly, "These people have come all the way from America to photograph you. You will do what they say, and you will keep doing it, until they tell you that they are finished."

Moskvina's onetime pair partner, Alexei Mishin, at the Olympics coaching 1998 European champion Alexei Yagudin, also demonstrated how to use the press to his advantage. An hour before his student was scheduled to skate, Mishin personally made the rounds of every TV broadcasting position to spread the word that Yagudin was running a fever, was being examined by the doctor as they spoke, and might withdraw. Mishin just thought they should know so that they could tell their audience in case Yagudin didn't perform well.

In the first days of the Olympics, the eventual winner of the men's event, Russia's Ilia Kulik, found himself without a coach to play the media on his behalf, as Tatiana Tarasova was busy putting out the fires sparked by her most volcanic student, Pasha Grishuk. But the twenty-year-old Leonardo DeCaprio look-alike proved himself more than capable of charming them on his own. As the first Russian to arrive in Nagano, Kulik had the story-hungry press all to himself. He joked that he came early "to get the best room in the Russian apartment at the Olympic village," then casually added that the back injury that kept him out of the European Championship was perfectly healed now, and his skating was terrific, just great. Did everyone see the triple axel he landed? He was ready to win.

Another skater to benefit from the first-to-arrive edge was America's Tara Lipinski. Unlike teammates Michelle Kwan and Nicole Bobek, who stayed at their Lake Arrowhead, California, training site until shortly before their event began, Tara didn't want to miss a moment of the Olympic experience she'd dreamed about since she was a toddler. She not only marched proudly and giddily in the opening ceremonies, she also attended several of the official practices in both the main and auxiliary rinks, where, with the absence of other American ladies, she had the world press all to herself. And Tara took full advantage of the opportunity.

The moment she stepped onto the ice, taking off her skate-guards and neatly laying them on the barrier, a plethora of cameras seemed to materialize from every corner of the rink. In the silence of an unfilled arena, each click of a shutter or buzz of a zoom lens testified to yet another electronic eye scrutinizing the diminutive defending world champion. Nor did Tara disappoint her observers.

Apparently oblivious to the cameras, she skated her programs without a single error, putting in every triple jump, every triple/triple combination, smiling with delight all the while. After the practice, a crowd of reporters clamored for a quote from the self-possessed teen. Her coach, Richard Callaghan, didn't want her to be bothered, and offered to field the questions himself. Tara said no. This was her show;

this was her time; this was her dream Olympics. She would be happy to chat with the press.

In contrast, 1995 U.S. champion Nicole Bobek and 1996 world champion Michelle Kwan arrived at the Olympics relatively late, and withdrew into virtual isolation. By the time Bobek started her first practice session, the cameras were focusing on Lipinski and Kwan. This seemed to leave Bobek at loose ends, tying and retying her skates. At one point, she performed a perfect short program, but then fell down for twenty minutes straight on every triple jump she tried.

The last medal favorite to arrive was Russia's Irina Slutskaya. Her late arrival prompted Elena Tchaikovskaya, coach of Slutskaya's Russian rival, Maria Butyrskaya, to tell any member of the media who was willing to listen that Slutskaya's coach was deliberately hiding Irina so that judges (and the press) wouldn't see how much weight the nineteen-year-old had gained since the European Championship.

In contrast to Bobek, Michelle skated well on her first practice, despite the cameras that, as they had for Tara, bled out of the woodwork and into her face. But when she wasn't on the ice, Michelle might as well not have been at the Olympics at all. Not only did she miss the opening ceremonies, (doctor's orders—she needed more time to rest a hairline fracture to her foot) she also declined to stay with the other skaters at the Athletes' Village. Her coach, Frank Carroll, maintained that it was Michelle's choice to spend her time in Nagano at a private apartment with her family, as the Athletes' Village was too noisy and distracting. He also said that he and Michelle had off-ice work to do, and it was better for them to be in close proximity.

For Michelle and Nicole, it appeared that the Olympics were just another international competition—fly in, skate, fly out again. Only Tara took full advantage of what could well be a once-in-a-lifetime opportunity. Though she did leave Nagano for the privacy of Osaka after the opening ceremonies (Rosalynn Sumners applauded the decision, explaining that in 1984 she'd stayed for the whole Games, and by the time the ladies' long program rolled around, she was exhausted), she returned to cheer on her training partner, Todd Eldredge, in the men's event, sitting in the stands with her teammates and later sharing a room with the 1998 world junior dance champion, Jessica Joseph, in the Athletes' Village.

In the end, the two teenage American world champions' Olympic experiences could be read conclusively in the presentation of their respective long programs. Michelle Kwan skated cautiously, slowly, executing every jump with deliberate precision and care, with little nonchoreographed emotion beyond a fear of falling. Her entourage, the media-dubbed "Team Kwan," had been so resolved to protect their ward from the press—Carroll boasted that Michelle read no newspaper accounts of either herself or the other competitors—that they practically locked the princess in a soundproof, airtight bubble. Michelle had no idea what was going on in Nagano other than what she was told by those forming a human cordon around her. When Michelle stepped on the ice to perform her long program, she did exactly what she'd been told to do—by her coach, by her

dad, by her choreographer, and by her agent. She skated with the weight of everyone's—including the media's—expectations that she was a shoo-in for the gold. The weight visibly slowed her down.

She didn't want to fall; she didn't want to disappoint; she wanted to do what was expected of her. And so, under the guidance of "Team Kwan," Michelle did not do the triple toe loop/triple toe loop combination that might have raised her technical mark close to that of Tara, who performed a more difficult triple loop/triple loop. Instead, as she was told to, Michelle played it safe. And, in a sport where every fraction of a fraction of a point counts, the trepidation cost her.

In contrast, Tara was skating for no one except herself— a fact made obvious when, in response to the question of how many triple/triple combinations she intended to do, coach Callaghan replied, "It's up to Tara." She'd watched the other skaters with the trained eye of a seasoned competitor and knew exactly what she had to do. She knew that it was up to her whether or not to do it. When Lipinski stepped on the ice, after weeks of skating her program perfectly under the watchful eye of every reporter in the world, she was ready to seize her moment. She outjumped Kwan. She outraced Kwan. But most of all, she outradiated Kwan, her joy lighting up the arena in a sparkle of nonchoreographed emotion that Michelle managed to achieve only once, when she burst into tears of relief at the conclusion of her program. (Trying to drag a bitter quote out of the always gracious Kwan, an NBC reporter at the

ALONG WITH A MULTITUDE OF COACHING CHANGES, NICOLE BOBEK HAS ALSO SUFFERED A BIZARRE SERIES OF HEALTH PROBLEMS. AMONG THEM: A STRAINED BACK, AN ALLERGIC REACTION TO ANESTHESIA DURING AN APPENDECTOMY THAT SENT HER TO INTENSIVE CARE, MONONUCLEOSIS, A CHIPPED BONE, A SPIKED RIGHT KNEE, AND A DOG BITE TO THE NECK. DAYS BEFORE THE 1999 NATIONALS, NICOLE WITHDREW, SUFFERING FROM AN OVARIAN CYST.

Golden Gala following the Olympics spent so much time asking over and over if Kwan felt angry about losing the gold medal that finally her agent, Shep Goldberg, stood up at the back of the room and asked, "If she says 'yes,' can we leave?")

Obviously, their painstaking courting of the media was not the sole factor that propelled Lipinski, Kulik, Kazakova and Dmitriev, and Grishuk and Platov to the gold. All the press conferences in the universe would have been futile without exemplary programs to back them up. Yet skating judges are human beings and cannot help but be affected by the persistent repetition from the media that so-and-so skated great today, so-and-so landed a triple/triple, so-and-so landed a quad, so-and-so looks like a winner.

And television, of course, has its own interest in creating stars even before the actual competition begins. After all, 1994's Nancy and Tonyapalooza earned block-buster ratings only because of the story that took place before the skating, not during it. In 1998, CBS hyped the Kwan/Lipinski rivalry before Michelle even set foot in Japan, interrupting coverage of their other events to show Tara grinning her way through practice after practice.

The idea is to generate interest before the contest. If viewers are interested in personalities, then they'll tune in for the contest, rooting for their favorite person, regardless of athletic execution. This phenomenon is

illustrated by the fact that Lipinski's victory over Kwan is still being ardently debated, despite the former's visibly surpassing the latter on every objective technical scale. But beacuse Kwan has a following of loyal fans, there were enough non-objective observers to stir up a debate.

Then, once television has created its stars, it can quickly channel them into other made-for-TV projects—pro competitions, prime-time specials, and tours—to capitalize on the popularity the producers themselves generated. It's a win/win situation for everyone concerned: the television networks, the skaters, and ultimately, skating itself.

THE STORY OF THE LADIES' IN NAGANO COULD BE READ ON THE FACES OF ITS COMPETITORS. IN THE END, THE ETHEREAL, SPIRITUAL MICHELLE KWAN (OPPOSITE) COULD NOT OVER-POWER THE SHEER ENERGY, EXUBER-ANCE, AND JOY OF HIGH-JUMPING TARA LIPINSKI (LEFT).

GETTING THERE

In 1994, 1984 Olympic dance champions Jayne Torvill and Christopher Dean could only earn third place behind a pair of younger competitors. In 1998, seventeen- year-old Michelle Kwan, a mere two years after winning the World Title, also found herself relegated to runner-up status behind a younger skater.

Some skaters, like 1998 Olympic champion Tara Lipinski, seem to step in front of the television cameras as soon as they strap on their first pair of skates. One month after her twelfth birthday, Tara became the youngest-ever gold medal winner at the 1994 U.S. Olympic Festival. The media fell in love with her, comparing the miniature pixie to everyone from Shirley Temple to Mary Lou Retton. They decided, then and there, that Tara Lipinski would be a star. It didn't matter that, the following year, their favorite to win the U.S. junior ladies' title only finished second. Taramania rolled on. It didn't matter that, in 1996, the little girl who allegedly never made a mistake placed out of the medals, in fifth place, at the World Junior Championship and, after two falls in the short program, fifteenth at the World Senior Championship (no American girl, outside of the qualifying group, had ever finished that low). Still, the media drums pounded, the press kits arrived, and the now fourteen-year-old, four-foot-eight-inch (142cm) Tara did not disappoint. In 1997, barely three years after America first learned to spell her name, she won the U.S. Championship, the Champions' Series final,

and the World Championship over the defending champion and former favorite, sixteen-year-old Michelle Kwan.

Kwan herself had made quite a media splash as a twelve-year-old in 1993, when she finished sixth at the U.S. Championship. Only ninth in the junior division a year earlier, Kwan told of waiting until coach Frank Carroll was out of town before disobeying his instructions and sneaking away to take the test that qualified her to compete as a senior. The story instantly became a fixture in the growing Kwan legend—except for one point no one has yet addressed or explained. In order to take the senior free-skating test, every contender needs to present a USFSA form signed by their club officer and their coach. Otherwise the test isn't valid. If she was disobeying Carroll's instructions, who signed her form?

One year after assuming the title of skating's newest child star, Kwan won the World Junior Championship and finished second at the Nationals. In any other year, her finish would have qualified her to compete at the 1994 Olympic Games. But 1994 was also the year of "Kardigan"—the skating world's nickname for the Kerrigan/Harding incident.

AT THE 1997 U.S. CHAMPIONSHIP, KWAN (OPPOSITE) FALTERED AND FELL, WHILE LIPINSKI (RIGHT) STAYED UP AND WON THE NATIONAL TITLE. AT THE 1998 U.S. CHAMPIONSHIP, IT WAS LIPINSKI WHO TOOK A FALL IN THE SHORT PROGRAM, AND KWAN WHO WON THE GOLD. ONLY AT THE OLYMPICS DID BOTH LADIES SKATE CLEAN PROGRAMS, SETTING THE STAGE FOR ONE OF THE TIGHTEST, MOST EXCITING CONTESTS IN OLYMPIC HISTORY.

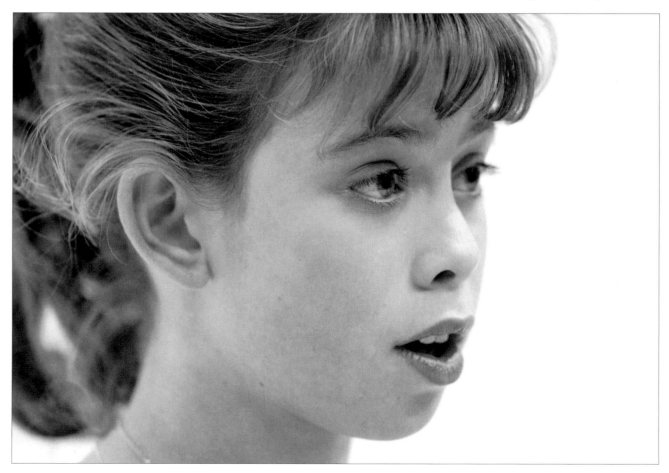

Nancy Kerrigan and Tonya Harding represented the U.S. at the Olympics. Kwan went to Norway as an alternate. Although she was within her rights to sue for a spot on the team, officials from the International Olympic Committee (IOC) and the USFSA convinced Kwan to lie low, arguing that she was still young and would have another chance. Besides, removing Harding from the U.S. team would mean holding a hearing on-site and having to fly every witness involved with the case from America to Lillehammer.

Kwan's second-place finish at the Nationals allowed her to compete at the subsequent World Champion-ship, where, as the only U.S. representative (Nicole Bobek was eliminated in the qualifying round), she finished eighth. A year later, just as they would one day with Tara, the media ordained Kwan the favorite for the 1995 U.S. title—a fact no one shared with Bobek, who won the title and, weeks later, the bronze medal at the World Championship. Kwan finished a spot behind, in fourth place, after skating the best performance of her career to that date. But in 1995, Kwan's best was not good enough. Judges thought she looked—and skated—too young.

So, for the 1995–1996 season, the ponytailed teenager from Torrance, California, transformed herself into the biblical temptress Salome. At the 1996 Worlds in Edmonton, Canada, Kwan also skated her best. This time, it was good enough for the title. In only her third World Championship, she captured the gold. Then, in 1997, Lipinski, on her way to shattering nearly every standing record, took just two tries to accomplish the same feat. Both young women managed to make it look easy.

However, for the majority of skaters, the road to

medals, fame, and prize money doesn't unroll in the blink of an eye. The road to even qualifying for, much less winning, an international event can be as choppy as a local rink's ice after a public session, with hurdles ranging from personal to financial to medical standing in the way.

PARENTS

For a few contestants, the hardships begin on day one—because they don't really want to skate. Dan Hollander, 1996 and 1997 U.S. bronze medalist, wanted to be a roller-skater, but the ice rink was closer to his Huntington Woods, Michigan, home,

HOPING TO REINFORCE HER IMAGE AS A "WOMAN AMONG LITTLE GIRLS," MARIA BUTYRSKAYA (RIGHT), IN 1998, POSED FOR THE RUSSIAN EDITION OF PLAYBOY. THE PICTURES, SHE EXPLAINED, WERE TASTEFUL, ARTISTIC, AND NOT FULLY NUDE. THAT SAME YEAR, TWO-TIME OLYMPIC CHAMPION KATARINA WITT POSED FOR THE AMERICAN VERSION OF PLAYBOY, WHILE HER COUNTRY-WOMAN, TANJA SZEWCZENKO, GRACED THE COVER OF THE GERMAN EDITION.

so his mom took him there instead. Alexei Urmanov, 1994 Olympic champion, remembers "crying the entire way to the rink" at age four, while 1998 world silver medalist Irina Slutskaya's mother reveals that her daughter used to "go into hysterics" at the mention of having to go skate. Yulia Lavrenchuk, 1997 Ukrainian champion and European bronze medalist, admits that she began skating at age five because "my parents forced me. In the beginning, they had to stuff me inside the rink while I was crying." Czech champion Lenka Kulovana adds that it took her eight years before she actually grew to enjoy skating, while 1979 world pair champion Tai Babilonia summarizes her early experience succinctly: "I hated it." Rumanian champion Cornel Gheorghe's mother used to bribe him with candy to get him to stay on the ice. Lithuania's Povilas

Vanagas received an even stronger incentive: during the days when Lithuania was part of the Soviet Union, the six-time men's champion was offered a choice—either fulfill his national service to the U.S.S.R. by getting drafted into the Soviet army or switch to ice dancing. Shrugs Vanagas, "I didn't want to dance. But I had no choice."

Yet even a child dying to get onto the ice requires a great deal of assistance along the way. And before the sponsors come a-knocking, initial support inevitably must come from the parents.

Hungarian champion and 1997 European silver medalist Krisztina Czako's father, Gyorgy, himself a three-time Hungarian champion, made his daughter's first pair of skates himself when she was just eleven months old. Since there is no ice time available in Hungary on the weekends, the Czakos drive to rinks in Austria and Slovakia to make sure Krisztina has a place to train.

It's a situation similar to that of 1997 German champion Eva-Marie Fitze. While her mother works in a boutique to support Eva-Marie's skating, her dad stays home and drives his daughter thirty miles (48km) each way to Munich. There, Eva-Marie trains at a rink built for the 1991 World Championship. Because the planners constructing the rink wanted to make sure it wasn't taken over by hockey players after the competition, they purposely designed it to be all glass. Hockey players can't practice there for fear of smashing the walls, so Germany's figure skaters have the ice all to themselves.

However, constantly chauffeuring one child around can take its toll on the rest of the family. Russian champion Maria Butyrskaya regretfully concedes that because her mother was always so busy with Maria's skating, Maria's brother, who is seven years

IN 1999, EVA-MARIE FITZE (LEFT) UPSET TANJA SZEWCZENKO, THE COMEBACK-KID OF 1998, TO WIN THE GERMAN NATIONAL TITLE.

younger, had to stay home alone and take care of himself. As a result, "He has had a very hard time finding himself in life." Ruth Eldredge, mother of 1996 world champion Todd Eldredge, says of her daily drive to a rink two hours away from their home in Chatham, Massachusetts, "We spent so much time on the road, I never saw the rest of the family much. It was just Todd all day long. He'd go to school for a few hours and then we're off to a rink. He was eating in the car, doing homework in the car with the light on at night; it was totally bizarre."

At age ten, Todd moved to Philadelphia to be closer to his coach, Richard Callaghan. Since then, Todd has followed him to Colorado Springs, San Diego, and Detroit, picking up various titles along the way: 1985 U.S. novice; 1987 U.S. junior; 1988 world junior; 1990, 1991, 1995, 1997, and 1998 U.S. senior; and 1996 world champion.

Stories of skaters moving away from home at a terribly young age dominate the sport. Lisa Ervin, 1993 U.S. silver medalist, was eight when her local coach moved. Lisa and her parents traveled to Cleveland for a tryout with 1960 Olympic champion-turned-coach Carol Heiss Jenkins. Jenkins adored Lisa and informed the Ervins, "You have a problem. You have a very talented child, and I want to coach her." Lisa's parents couldn't move for the sake of skating, so they sent their nine-year-old to board with another family.

But when faced with relocating her daughter, Tara, alone, Pat Lipinski said no. She didn't want someone else raising her child. So for the sake of Tara's career, Pat left husband Jack in their Sugar Land, Texas, home while she and Tara moved to Newark, Delaware, and then Detroit.

In Russia, where the housing situation remains a great deal more critical than in the United States, Irina Slutskaya's parents did the inconceivable and gave up a hard-to-find three-room apartment so that they could move into a one-room studio closer to where Irina trains.

Once so many basic sacrifices have been made, it becomes natural for parents to want to become even more involved in their child's skating career. Some even choose to take on the role of their child's nutritionist. Peggy Fleming's mother, minutes before Peggy was set to take the ice at the 1966 U.S. Nationals, insisted that Peggy had to have macaroni and cheese. Unable to find the dish at any restaurant, Peggy, her mother, and her coach, Carlo Fassi, drove all over the city, stopping at every possible eatery until they finally found it.

Other parents contribute to their child's skating by becoming music editors, costume designers, psychiatrists, and even coaches.

Yuka Sato won the gold in her home country of Japan while under the tutelage of her father and mother. Second at those championships—and creating quite a controversy by ripping off her silver medal while standing on the podium—was Surya Bonaly of France. An uncontrovertibly gifted athlete who won the 1987 World Novice Tumbling Championship as well as the 1991 World Junior Figure Skating Championship, Surya is coached by her adoptive mother, Suzanne—a physical education teacher who has absolutely no skating experience. Though Surya has taken lessons from many coaches over the years, Suzanne has always had the final word in every discussion. Arguably as a result of her mother's refusal to permit Surya a full-time, professional coach, her daughter's international ranking has slipped from second in the world from 1993 to 1995 to fifth in 1996 to failing to make the world team in 1997 to losing her French national title in 1998.

Tamara Moskvina, 1969 world pair silver medalist and coach of 1998 Olympic champions Kazakova and Dmitriev, has a simple policy regarding skating parents at the ice rink: "I do not go into their place of work to check if they are doing it correctly; they should not come to mine." A workable policy to enforce in Russia, where skating lessons are free, as long as the child is judged to exhibit potential.

In America, however, according to Moskvina's ex-pair partner, Alexei Mishin, coach of 1994 Olympic champion Urmanov and 1998 world

bronze medalist Evgeny Plushenko, "Parents pay for lessons, and parents want results right away. Axel! Triple jump! [A lesson is] twenty minutes and forget it. It's like a Ford factory. Not the way to make champions."

In Russia, the first year of a skater's training includes no jump lessons whatsoever. Instead, aspiring champions are taught correct stroking technique, backward and forward crossovers—a skill judges most often note as lacking in Western skaters—and muscle control. They are taught how to distinguish and regulate every muscle in their body so that when it comes time to finally learn a jump, it's only a matter of telling each muscle what to do. Russians don't even bother teaching pair overhead lifts until the boy is fully grown, arguing that

there's no point teaching him what he'll only have to relearn later, when he reaches his final height, and that in the meantime, lifting too early risks serious injuries.

In Russia, coaches can get away with teaching skills at their own pace because they have no one to answer to. In America, a coach who fails to produce quick results could find himself without a student— or an income. In America, because parents pay the bills, parents call the proverbial tune. And, many argue, that's exactly how it should be, considering the money necessary just to get a young skater started.

FINANCIAL

First, there is the cost of skates. A custom-made pair, with specialized freestyle, figure, or dance blades, can cost close to $1,000. Money for costumes—sewn, beaded, and embroidered by hand— is another $1,000. Next is the money for coaches. The more established ones charge more than $60 an hour. There is also money for private ice, plane tickets to competitions for both skater and coach, hotel charges for skater and coach, off-ice dance lessons, music editing, and physical therapy. A novice or junior competitor could easily spend $30,000 a year on skating; a senior international competitor could spend $100,000.

Tai Babilonia's father worked two jobs in order to earn enough money to keep his daughter skating. Three-time U.S. silver medalist Lisa-Marie Allen needed her grandparents to help her divorced mother pay the bills. And Todd Eldredge' entire town joined in the effort to keep him on the ice.

Following his 1985 U.S. novice title, Todd's parents came to the unhappy realization that they could no longer afford to keep their very talented son skating. That's when the town of Chatham, Massachusetts, pitched in to help. Neighbors went door to door and held summer clambakes to solicit donations. The Chatham Youth Hockey League set up a fund to help with expenses. Laughs Todd, "I'm probably the only figure skater ever supported by a hockey team."

Their town came through for 1997 Canadian pair champions Marie-Claude Savard-Gagnon and Luc Bradet, too. The two were next-door neighbors living in a small town, Baie-St-Paul, in Quebec, and just going to the local ice rink to hang out when, at ages twelve and fourteen, a coach spotted them and decided the pair had potential. Neither Marie-Claude nor Luc's family could afford to cover all the costs of a serious skating career, so their community pitched in to help. Every year, the local club presents a skating show, the proceeds from which go to support the pair.

Those without such an option, however, often need to resort to even more creative financing techniques. Calla Urbanski and Rocky Marval, 1992 and 1993 U.S. pair champions, earned their nickname "the Waitress and the Truck Driver" by working at those blue-collar jobs while training for the Olympics. Karen Courtland (1994 U.S. bronze medalist) and former partner David Goodman, in pairs, performed at children's parties as painted clowns, using acrobatic lifts they carried over from skating. Rudy Galindo, 1996 U.S. men's champion, lived in a trailer park with his mother, pedaled a creaky bike to the rink, and bummed free lessons from his sister, Laura. Aspiring hopeful Larry Holiday took frugality a step further, and just lived in his car while attempting to qualify for the 1994 Olympics.

He didn't make it.

PHYSICAL

Still, all the money in the world does no good when the hurdle in the way of a skater striking gold is of a physical nature.

Two weeks before the 1992 U.S. Championship, a qualifier for the Olympics, ice dancer April Sargent-Thomas, suffered a ruptured ovarian cyst, began hemorrhaging, and had to be rushed to emergency surgery. Her partner, Russ Witherby, was convinced their Olympic dream was over. Yet six days after leaving the hospital, April disobeyed doctors' orders and returned to the ice. With Nationals

only a week away, she could barely move. The team had to start all over again, listening to their music and wracking their brains for a way to change this step and alter that lift so that April wouldn't be hurt. When they skated their free dance at Nationals, it was the first time they ever performed it from beginning to end since April's surgery. The team finished in first place.

Tanja Szewczenko, 1994 world bronze medalist, began suffering foot injuries soon after winning her medal because she had performed in too many exhibitions. Szewczenko's coach wanted her to drop the exhibitions and rest for competition. Tanja dropped her coach instead and moved to a new rink. She missed the 1996–1997 season because of a life-threatening blood virus that doctors, at first, could not diagnose. After a year of inaction, still fragile from weekly blood transfusions, Tanja returned to the ice in 1997, regained her German title, and qualified for the Champions' Series final where, after an impeccable performance, she finished a close second behind defending champion Tara Lipinski. She also won the short program at the 1998 Europeans, finishing third overall. Arriving at the 1998 Olympics, Tanja was considered one of the favorites for the bronze. Unfortunately, in Nagano, she caught the flu and regretfully withdrew from the ladies' event.

For France's Laurent Tobel, though, it was a physical problem that first drove him not away, but *to* the rink. As a child his immune system was weak, and he needed to be in a cold environment. (It was a situation reminiscent of 1984 Olympic champion Scott Hamilton who, at age two, contracted a mysterious illness that caused him to stop growing. A special diet and exercise were recommended as treatment, and the cold air of skating was thought to be good

for his lungs. As he began to train, Scott also began growing again.) But for Laurent, it was a converse physical problem that almost drove him out of skating. When he was fourteen years old, he grew eighteen inches (46cm) in one year. The acceleration weakened his bones, caused shinsplints and knee injuries, and wreaked havoc with his balance. He had to relearn every skating move, from stroking to spinning to jumping, before he finally stopped growing when he reached six feet two inches (188cm). Citing his hulking size, many urged Laurent to give up skating. (American Karen Kwan, sister of Michelle, was watching Laurent at a competition in France and reportedly joked, "There's a monster on the ice. I'm afraid he'll eat me.") But the two-time French junior silver medalist vowed to make a comeback. As a last-minute addition to the 1997 World Team after the withdrawal of Philippe

Candeloro, Laurent skated a comical "Pink Panther" program, more exhibition than competition, that inspired a standing ovation from the crowd.

At the same World Championship, another French skater, Sophie Moniotte, was attempting a comeback of her own. She and partner Pascal Lavanchy had been as high as second in ice dance in 1994. But prior to the 1996 season, Sophie was practicing twizzles when her blade got caught in the ice. She turned; her foot didn't. Sophie describes it as being "in a Bugs Bunny cartoon. I go round and round." She broke her ankle and tore a ligament; it took five months to fully heal, and Sophie was forced to stay off the ice for almost a year. Sophie and Pascal missed the entire 1995–1996 season, and although Sophie watched the Worlds on

television, Pascal refused to. In their absence, the French ice dance title was won by Marina Anissina and Gwendal Peizerat. When Sophie and Pascal returned to competition in 1996–1997, they earned only second place at the French Nationals. However, determined to "prove we're alive and we kept on working," Sophie and Pascal went on to win the bronze medal at the 1997 Europeans over their closest rivals.

While Sophie and Pascal were missing in action, their spot on the world podium was taken by a pair of Canadians, Shae-Lynn Bourne and Victor Kraatz. The 1996 and 1997 world bronze medalists were no strangers to injury themselves. In 1992, Shae-Lynn collided with another skater in practice and fractured her skull. Doctors told her that if she ever hit

the exact same spot again, she could end up a vegetable. Shae-Lynn listened politely, then went right back out onto the ice to win the junior dance title.

A more serious cranial injury struck Russian pair skater Elena Bereznaia. She and her partner, Latvia's Oleg Shliakhov, were practicing side-by-side camel spins for an exhibition performance at the Latvian Nationals when Oleg's blade struck Elena on the side of the head. At first she didn't realize she'd been hit by the blade; she thought it was the boot. But then she felt herself slowly starting to sink down, as something warm and sticky slithered down her face. She stepped off the ice, still feeling nothing. Her coaches and Oleg told her she was fine, that she was just in shock and might need a few stitches for the bloody cut on her head. Ambulance drivers took her to the hospital, then left her in the waiting room. It was while she was sitting there that Elena began to feel progressively worse. By the time a nurse came to ask her name and where she lived, Elena couldn't remember or articulate the information. She was wearing contact lenses, but when she tried to tell that to the nurse, she couldn't come up with the right words. When the doctors realized that her skull had been fractured, she was rushed into surgery. Lying on the table, Elena looked up to see her doctor's hands start shaking when he was told that the girl under his knife was a world-class athlete and that he'd better not make the same mistake as with his last patient, who had just died.

When Elena woke up after brain surgery, she couldn't speak or move the right side of her body. The delicate eighteen-year-old had lived away from home since the age of twelve, when a Soviet Sports Committee visited her Siberian hometown and decreed that she would be good for pairs; now she wanted her mother. But Tatiana Bereznaia was trapped in a hell of her own. Since the breakup of the Soviet Union had legislated Latvia an independent country, a Russian citizen like Elena's mother needed a visa to go there. It took four days before her paperwork was processed.

In the meantime, Elena had Oleg's mother to deal with. She and Oleg descended on the hospital immediately after Elena's surgery, urging her to "stop lazing around and get out of bed" so that Oleg and Elena could compete at the Champions' Series final and the Worlds. When Elena's mother finally arrived in Latvia and saw the condition her daughter was in, barely able to move or speak, she put her foot down and announced that there would be no talk of skating until her child was fully recovered.

Horrified when she was told she might not be able to skate for up to six months, Elena resolved to get back on the ice as soon as possible—because she could think of nothing else she wanted to do with her life. Upon her return to St. Petersburg, where she and Oleg had trained with Tamara Moskvina, therapy helped Elena regain mobility on her right side, although she still had trouble with small motor skills like touching her fingers together. Her speech also returned, though with a slight stutter and a faint accent that Russians mistake for an American one.

Her new partner, Anton Sikharulidze, was someone Elena knew from before her accident, and she trusted him, despite the fact that, at the 1996 Cup of Russia competition, a horrified Anton dropped a still-recovering Elena out of a lift and onto her head. Moving in with his family in St. Petersburg, Elena became romantically involved with Anton, though Anton cautioned, "At our young age, it is too early to speak words like 'love.'"

But in 1997, it wasn't too early to speak words like "contenders." Despite having skated together for less than a year, Elena and Anton finished third at the Europeans, ahead of teammates and world champions Shishkova and Naumov. They also finished second at the Russian Nationals, ahead of 1996 European champions Kazakova and Dmitriev. At the 1997 Worlds in Lausanne, Elena and Anton were in third place after the short program. If they skated a clean long, they had a chance to win the World Championship.

It wasn't to be. Stepping onto the ice, the team that no one bet would make it so far so fast was suddenly struck by nerves. Anton discovered that fear had paralyzed his muscles. He couldn't raise his hand and ended up falling twice on jumps, while Elena went down on two throws. Disgusted with himself, Anton stormed out of the kiss-and-cry area, leaving Elena and Moskvina to sit and wait for the marks that would plunge them from third to ninth place.

By the following season, the "miracle couple" was back on track, winning both the Champions' Series final and the 1998 European Championship, as well as a controversial silver medal (Anton fell in the short program, and both took a tumble toward the end of their long) at the 1998 Olympics, and finally, the 1998 World Pair Championship.

PARTNERS

Despite a few stumbles along the way, Elena Bereznaia is lucky to have found such a compatible partner after only two tries. For numerous skaters, the search for that perfect dance or pair partner can

be excruciating—even when you're an Olympic gold medalist like Russia's Artur Dmitriev.

Dmitriev and partner Natalia Mishkutenok won Olympic gold in 1992, Olympic silver in 1994, and two world titles. But Natalia, suffering back problems as a result of such agile, spine-twisting signature moves as "Natalia's Spin" (at the 1992 Worlds, the Soviet team doctor covertly predicted, "That girl will be in a wheelchair by the time she's thirty"), wanted to retire from competition. Artur did not. And so the hunt was on to find him another partner.

Artur recalls, "I try out with maybe four or five good people before I skate with Oksana [Kazakova]. It took one try only."

At their first World Championship in 1996, all the pundits' eyes were on Oksana to see if she could match up to her much-medaled partner. When the fresh team finished out of the medals, in fifth place, the blame was laid squarely on Oksana's shoulders, despite the fact that Artur made his share of mistakes, including losing his center on a spin and skidding dangerously close to Oksana.

By the following season, it became clear that it was Artur who now needed to hustle to keep up with his rapidly improving partner. In the short program at Skate America '96, it was Artur who missed the side-by-side triple toe loop, Artur who dropped Oksana out of a lift, and Artur who tripped and fell flat on his stomach during the footwork sequence. It was also Artur who, at the 1997 Worlds, missed the triple toe loop, leaving the team to finish third. Artur and Oksana again finished third at the 1998 Russian Nationals, and their chance for Olympic gold seemed to be slipping away daily.

Yet, as coach Moskvina predicted, "Artur is very knowledgeable in how to skate in the Olympics. Experienced people know when to start really working. He is collecting his strengths, his desires, his responsibilities for that moment in the Olympics."

True to Tamara's word, Artur Dmitriev arrived in Nagano looking trim and healthy, thanks to having sworn off "partying" (a word he preferred the press use in place of "drinking") for the period leading up

to the Games. After he and Oksana won their gold medal, however, Artur promptly disappeared, leaving Oksana to skate many of their exhibition practices alone. The moratorium on "partying" was definitely over.

While Dmitriev found the perfect partner at his very own rink, America's Brian Wells had to drive across the country looking for the right girl. At five feet four inches (163cm), Brian first skated pairs with his sister, Ann-Marie. They represented the U.S. at Junior Worlds in 1988 and 1989. Then Ann-Marie outgrew him. Brian's next partner, Laura Murphy, was just the right size at the age of thirteen, but eventually she also grew too big. So in 1994, Brian hit the road, and seemingly everywhere he turned, he heard one name: twelve-year-old Shelby Lyons. The novice-level Shelby was actively looking for a dance partner; she had no interest in skating pairs. For two months, Brian badgered the Lyons family with telephone calls. Finally, he convinced Shelby to give pairs a whirl. It took her a month to pass the USFSA tests qualifying her to compete in senior pairs. A year later, they finished fourth in the United States, and the year after that, Brian and the little girl who had no interest in skating pairs qualified for the World Team.

Artur's and Brian's stories are typical in that men searching for a partner tend to find one with relative ease. At the partner tryout sponsored every year by the Professional Skaters' Association (PSA), the number of girls who show up looking for partners tend to outnumber the boys fifteen to one. It's the women in skating who can spend months, sometimes years, seeking a match.

Eve Chalom looked all over the United States for an ice dance partner before a coach introduced her to Mathew Gates of England. In order to skate with Eve, Mathew had to relocate to America and move in with the Chaloms, who agreed to pay all his training and living expenses. It was, Eve's parents admit, like taking on another child, both financially and emotionally. For the first few years of their partnership, Mathew lived in a room once belonging to Eve's Yale-bound brother, Adam. But in 1996, Eve and Mathew decided there was such a thing as too much togetherness on and off the ice, and Mathew moved into his own apartment, still subsidized by the Chaloms. Eve's family also helped Mathew establish legal status in the United States. In February 1996, Susan Chalom drove Mathew six hours through a raging ice storm to Toronto, where he was processed for permanent residency. Instead of waiting in line with the rest of the applicants, Mathew was treated like a celebrity and processed immediately. Although his green card came through in August, his lack of citizenship prevented Mathew and Eve from challenging for a spot on the 1998 U.S. Olympic team.

As international barriers crumble and skating becomes an increasingly viable enterprise to embark on, international partner searches are growing ever more commonplace.

Russia's Marina Anissina thought she'd found herself a perfect match when she and Ilya Averbukh won the World Junior Ice Dance Championship in 1990 and 1992. But 1992 was also the year Ilya fell in love with another ice dancer, Irina Lobatcheva, and left Marina to skate with his new girlfriend.

Devastated, Marina didn't skate for six months. Unable to find another partner in Russia, she took out her nicest stationary and wrote two letters overseas. The first was to Canada's Victor Kraatz. She gave it to a member of the Canadian team to pass on to Victor. He never responded. (According to Victor, however, he never received any letter, because he certainly would have replied if he had.) The second letter went to France's Gwendal

Peizerat, whom Marina had spied competing at Junior Worlds. Gwendal wrote back explaining that he had a commitment to skate one more meet with his current partner. Afterward, however, he would be very interested in trying out with Marina.

Clutching a three-month visitor's visa and speaking no French, Marina traveled alone to Paris. Although she and Gwendal decided immediately to skate together, Marina still had to return to Moscow and wait for the paperwork to be processed before she could return permanently to France. For most people, the process of becoming a French citizen takes five years. However, the French Skating Federation pushed the process through in only two and a half years for their 1996 and 1997 national champion so that Marina could represent France at the 1998 Olympics. Marina is now a dual citizen of France and Russia, though she admits, "In my heart, I am Russian."

This fact appears obvious to any spectator. A member of the press who was observing Marina's behavior at one skating function sniffed, "It would be nice if Marina at least pretended to act like a member of the French team, instead of spending all night sitting and chatting with the Russians."

National confusion aside, Marina's defection to France appears to have been the right choice—for her and for them. At the 1998 Olympics, Marina and Gwendal won the bronze medal ahead of Victor Kraatz and the partner he ended up skating with, Shae-Lynn Bourne, as well as Marina's former partner, Ilya Averbukh, and his wife, Irina Lobatcheva.

Another Russian Irina, Irina Rodnina, once suffered a setback similar to Marina Anissina's. Despite their winning four world pair titles and the 1972 Olympic gold, Irina Rodnina's partner, Alexei Ulanov, decided to break up the twosome. He'd fallen in love with Ludmila Smirnova and wanted to skate with her.

After a well-publicized nationwide search, Irina teamed up with Alexander Zaitsev. At their first World Championship, barely two minutes into their long program, the music stopped. Irina was convinced it was sabotage. She'd had a dream the night before that such a thing would happen, and determined that nothing would stop her from proving she was back with a vengeance, Irina and Alexander continued skating. The crowd began clapping, hoping to give them some sort of beat to work with. The referee blew his whistle. He tried to stop the team. Irina and Alexander kept skating. In the end, they skated away with the gold medal. Alexei Ulanov and his new partner, Ludmila Smirnova, finished second.

Irina Rodnina had proven that she could be a champion with any man. Then, as if to make sure this partner wouldn't get away from her as easily, Irina married him.

It is a trend the Russians have continued to this day: 1964 and 1968 Olympic pair champion Ludmila Belousova married partner Oleg Protopopov; 1976 Olympic dance champion

Ludmila Pakhomova married partner Alexandr Gorshkov; 1980 Olympic dance champion Natalia Linichuk married partner Gennadi Karpanosov; 1984 Olympic pair champion Elena Valova married partner Oleg Vasiliev; 1988 and 1994 Olympic pair champion Ekaterina Gordeeva married partner Sergei Grinkov; 1992 Olympic silver medalist Elena Bechke married partner Denis Petrov; 1992 Olympic dance champion Marina Klimova married partner Sergei Ponomarenko; 1994 Olympic dance silver medalist Maia Usova married partner Alexandr Zhulin; and 1996 European bronze dance medalist Irina Romanova married partner Igor Yaroshenko.

The key tenet to a successful pair or dance couple is that "two shall skate as one." It is a feat that can be accomplished only by many years of togetherness, and once achieved, it can be hard to surrender. Because of the amount of time necessary to fuse a successful pairs or dance team, some couples continue to perform together even after getting a divorce.

Valova and Vasiliev continued to compete for a few years after their divorce. She is now remarried. In retrospect, Vasiliev supposes that spending sixteen years exclusively in each other's company caused the two to confuse friendship with love. He told *International Figure Skating* magazine, "After we broke up, nothing changed in our friendship, so that is why nothing changed in our skating."

Bechke and Petrov not only continued to compete together, but also tour together with Stars on Ice, coach together in Virginia, and vacation together! Petrov says, "Sometimes we skate not so good, and people say, 'They skate bad because they're divorced.' It's not really true." Like Vasiliev, he thinks his relationship with Elena improved after their divorce.

Life, however, isn't quite as rosy for Maia Usova and Alexandr Zhulin. While residing in Lake Placid and training for the 1994 Olympics, "Sasha" Zhulin had an affair with another Russian skater, Oksana (later Pasha) Grishuk. Though Usova and Zhulin stayed together long enough to win the silver in

Lillehammer (behind, of all people, Grishuk and Evgeny Platov), they divorced soon after.

It was only then that the truth about so many of the Russian marriages began to come out.

In 1995, Zhulin admitted to *American Skating World*, "The reason we got married is not as you thought. Fifty percent of the couples married because we Russians had nothing. No money. Our couples were not married for love but survival. If we married, we could get an apartment from our federation. Apartments are scarce, so they would rather give one to a couple than two to singles."

In 1995, Maia was still insisting that their divorce was for the best. "Before, we were always together, practicing together, living together. It was very difficult. Now we skate together, but we live apart, and we're as good friends as we ever were."

Less than two years later they were living even further apart—Maia in Massachusetts, Sasha in Connecticut—but the professional relationship remains. Explains Sasha, "I don't know how we could skate together with anyone else. For me to change partners now and still try to work the same way would not be a good idea."

That sort of dedication to career over personal concerns is common among the ex-Soviets, but much harder to find in the West.

A few teams have tried to emulate the Russian model by getting married. Finnish 1995 world dance silver medalists Susanna Rahkamo and Petri Kokko are married, as are 1995 world pair champions Radka Kovarikova and Rene Novotny. American pair skaters Jenni Meno and Todd Sand fell in love at the 1992 Albertville Olympics (she was there with Scott Wendland, he with Natasha Kuchiki) and decided to skate together. They became engaged at the 1994 Olympics, won the U.S. Championship in early 1995, and married that summer. Teammates Elizabeth Punsalan and Jerod Swallow became dance partners in March 1989. Elizabeth had a crush on Jerod from the first time she met him, but she wasn't sure about his feelings for her and so said nothing. At a competition in Lake Placid, a window-shopping Liz saw a ruby antique ring that she absolutely fell in love with, but her mother felt it was too expensive. A month later, Liz saw the ring on Jerod's pinky finger. Her mother had bought it and sent it to him. But it wasn't until 1992 that the true significance of the ring became clear. Over dinner, Jerod handed Liz a card. "The time has come. We're right for each other. Be my wife." The ruby antique became an engagement ring.

An even smaller number of Western teams have managed to keep a partnership together after the personal relationship soured.

German 1997 world pair champions Mandy Wotzel and Ingo Steuer were still a couple off the ice when, at the 1994 Olympics, Mandy fell chin-first onto the ice and had the wind knocked out of her. The world watched as Ingo tenderly cradled her in his arms and carried her off. Since then, the couple has broken up, though they continue to share a house and two apartments in Chemnitz.

For Mandy and Ingo, skating was actually a way for the pair to reconnect as friends after the romantic estrangement. Having to see each other every day, put their arms around each other, and look into each other's eyes was the catalyst they needed to stop growling and reestablish a rapport.

But such happy-ending-complete-with-world-championship tales are an exception to the rule in the West, where both pair and dance teams break up at the drop of a hat.

"You have to kiss a lot of frogs before you find a prince" is Calla Urbanski's most quoted quip, and Calla knows the truth of it well. Taking up pairs skating at the ripe age of twenty-three, she went through four partners before teaming up with Rocky Marval in 1986. After three months together, the pair called it quits (for the first time). Calla went on to skate with Mark Naylor and finish fourth at the 1990 U.S. Championship. Rocky paired up with Maria Lako and they finished seventh at the same

event. That spring, Calla and Rocky tried skating together again. A surprise silver medal at the 1991 Nationals earned them a trip to Worlds and a top-ten international ranking. In 1992, while on tour after they won a national title, they split up for the second time because of personality problems. (Calla is intense, while Rocky is more laid back.) Practice sessions had a nasty tendency to disintegrate into clenched-teeth snarls, shrill discussions, and stony silences. Hoping to catapult a fresh start, Calla tried out with Scott Kurtilla while still on tour with Rocky, who tried out with Natasha Kuchiki, also partnerless after Todd Sand left her for Jenni Meno. Neither pairing worked out. By the fall of 1992, "the Waitress and the Truck Driver" were back on again. "Third time's the charm," both swore. In 1993, Calla was skating with Joe Mero, Rocky with Kuchiki. Neither one managed to qualify for the 1994 Olympic team, though Rocky came closer with a fourth-place photo-finish. Immediately after the Nationals, Calla announced her retirement from amateur skating. She would become a professional skater—with Rocky Marval. After all, fourth time's the charm...or is it the third?

Suzanne Semanick won the 1983 U.S. junior dance title with Alexander Miller, the 1987 and 1988 U.S. senior dance titles with Scott Gregory, and two U.S. bronze medals with Ron Kravette. Ron won the 1986 U.S. junior dance title with Colette Huber and two more U.S. bronze medals with Amy Webster. Jason Dungjen won the 1983

OPPOSITE: U.S. CHAMPIONS ELIZABETH PUNSALAN AND JEROD SWALLOW BURST ONTO THE INTERNATIONAL ICE-DANCING SCENE WITH THEIR UNCONVENTIONAL FREE DANCE, "THE RACE," WHEREIN BOTH PORTRAYED RACING CARS. HOWEVER, UPON SWITCHING COACHES TO IGOR SHPILBAND, THE PAIR, LIKE MOST OF SHPILBAND'S OTHER TEAMS, FELL INTO A "LATIN RUT."

LEFT: AMONG THOSE SKATERS NOT THRILLED WITH THE ISU'S NEW, PRO/AM FORMAT ARE U.S. CHAMPIONS CALLA URBANSKI AND ROCKY MARVAL. THE PAIR COMPLAIN THAT, DESPITE BEING READY, THEY NEVER RECEIVED A SINGLE INVITATION TO A COMPETITION DURING THE 1998–99 SEASON.

U.S. junior pair title with sister Susan, and skated a season with Karen Courtland before pairing up with Kyoko Ina to win the 1997 and 1998 U.S. Championships.

Or is it the second time that's the charm?

Renee Roca won the 1986 U.S. dance title with Donald Adair and the 1993 and 1995 titles with Gorsha Sur. Susan Wynne won the 1989 and 1990 U.S. dance titles with Joe Druar, then came back from the professional ranks to earn the 1993 and 1994 U.S. silvers with Russ Witherby.

In any case, the partner merry-go-round once prompted Tamara Moskvina to observe that it was ultimately pointless: "There is no improvement because always changing, changing, changing. It's back where you started."

The sporadic long-term partnerships that manage to survive in America are usually brother/sister

pairings, where blood is thicker than medals: 1948–1952 U.S. pair champs Karol and Peter Kennedy; 1963–1964 U.S. pair champs Judy and Jerry Fotheringill; 1965 U.S. pair champs Vivian and Ronald Joseph; 1966–1969 U.S. pair champs Cynthia and Ronald Kauffman; 1973 U.S. pair champs Melissa and Mark Militano (though she would go on to win the 1974 and 1975 U.S. pairs title with Johnny Johns); and 1981–1984 U.S pair champions and 1984 Olympic silver medalists Kitty and Peter Carruthers.

Then there are the special cases: Western skaters whose partnerships have lasted longer than some marriages. Christine Hough and Doug Ladret, 1988 Canadian pair champions, started skating together in 1984 and grew to be such close friends that, when Doug got married in the summer of 1995, Christine served as his "best man."

JoJo Starbuck and Ken Shelley began skating together as seven-year-olds. She recalls, "Before we started taking [lessons] from Mr. [John] Nicks, we were taught by another man who taught us ice dancing. We thought it was pretty silly. We used to laugh through the lesson. The coach used to walk off the ice. We couldn't be serious and we knew we were making him mad, so we decided to change coaches. We started taking lessons from this new man and we went immediately from ice dancing to pairs skating and we didn't even know the difference."

When John Nicks, with sister Jennifer, won the World Pair Championship in 1953, lifts were not a part of the program. So when it came to teaching JoJo and Ken how to do them, Nicks learned along with the kids. They began by having Ken try to lift JoJo off the piano in their dance studio. By 1968, the sixteen-year-olds from California proved good enough to earn a spot on the Olympic Team. By 1971, they won the world bronze medal, repeating the feat in 1972. Afterward, they headlined the Ice Capades for four years, were named Professional Skaters of the Year, were inducted into the U.S. Figure Skating Hall of Fame, and, as of 1997, were still competing—together—in the Legends Professional Championship.

As one of John Nicks' first pairs, JoJo expresses amazement that the tricks it took them years to figure out, Nicks taught to his next championship pair, Tai Babilonia and Randy Gardner, in a matter of months.

Tai and Randy were initially paired up as children to perform as Mr. and Mrs. Doolittle in a club show. Neither grade-schooler was ecstatic about holding hands with a member of the opposite sex, and had to be bribed with candy bars. By 1974, thirteen-year-old Tai and fifteen-year-old Randy became the youngest pair ever to make the World Team. In 1979, they were the first American pair to win the World Championship in twenty-nine years, although Randy's groin injury kept them from competing at the 1980 Olympics. The pair also toured with Ice Capades and—after a seven-year hiatus—competed at the first World Pro Championship. In 1998, they were celebrating thirty years of skating together while touring with *Champions on Ice.*

PAIRS SKATER JOHN NICKS, WHO, WITH HIS SISTER WON THE 1953 WORLD CHAMPIONSHIP, WENT ON TO A FANTASTIC CAREER AS A PAIRS COACH. HE HAS COACHED SEVERAL WINNING PAIRS, INCLUDING JO JO STARBUCK AND KEN SHELLEY, JENNI MENO AND TODD SAND, AND TAI BABILONIA AND RANDY GARDNER (PICTURED IN AN ON-ICE PRACTICE SESSION WITH NICKS).

PERSONAL

At the 1994 Olympics, much media fuss was made over the story of Oksana Baiul. Orphaned as a teen, she was unofficially adopted by her coach, Galina Zmievskaya, and with financial help from 1992 Olympic champion Viktor Petrenko, Oksana rose to win the World and Olympic championships. But a shortage of parents isn't the sole personal problem faced by some skaters. Canada's Kristy Sargeant thought her career was over when, at age seventeen, she became one.

Despite giving birth to a baby daughter, Triston, in 1992, and losing her pair-partner as a result, Kristy kept on skating. She tried singles for a while, emulating her older sister, Canadian champ Lisa Sargeant-Driscoll. When the chance came to return to pairs with 1992 Olympian Kris Wirtz, Kristy left Triston with her parents in Alberta and relocated to Quebec.

After competing at the 1994 Olympics, Kristy realized that no matter how hard it would be to train while having Triston living with her, it was even harder without her. She and Kris, who had become romantically involved since pairing up, brought Triston to live with them, and say that having the little girl around helps them take their mind off skating.

Having family around also helped U.S. ice dancers Punsalan and Swallow deal with the greatest personal tragedy of their career.

Mere days before they were scheduled to leave for the 1994 Olympics, Liz's mentally ill twenty-one-year-old brother, believing he was Jesus and his father was Satan, stabbed Dr. Ernesto Punsalan to death. Liz and Jerod rushed to Ohio for the funeral, missing four crucial days of training. They wondered whether they should even go to the Olympics. But, Jerod recalls, "Everyone in the family insisted that we compete." Liz's mother, sister, and two brothers traveled to Lillehammer to watch them skate, and the memory of how much joy Dr. Punsalan drew from seeing his daughter perform helped Liz and Jerod get through the difficult weeks.

Family also helped Michael Shmerkin weather some rough spots in his skating career. Misha's mother and father were so supportive, they even got a divorce so that he could compete.

Born in Odessa in the U.S.S.R., Misha trained alongside Viktor Petrenko and shared his coach, Galina Zmievskaya. A promising young skater, Misha was informed by the Soviet Skating Federation that if he intended to represent the U.S.S.R. internationally, he would have to do one little thing—stop being Jewish.

In the U.S.S.R., where Judaism is considered a nationality, a non-Russian or -Ukrainian could not be allowed to represent his country. To that end, Misha's Jewish parents divorced, and his mother married—on paper—a Russian family friend, who then passed his nationality onto his new stepson. Misha

went on to represent the U.S.S.R. at Junior Worlds and at the 1990 GosTeleRadio Championship in Odessa, where he won the short program over the future 1994 Olympic champion Alexei Urmanov.

Still, with the situation in the Soviet Union rowing more and more unpredictable, Misha's parents, who never officially remarried—Misha teases them about "living in sin"—decided to immigrate to Israel. Misha thought his skating career was over, though he does credit Zmievskaya with being supportive: "She let me skate at her rink until the very last day before I left."

Once in Israel, Misha prayed at the Western Wall, asking God to make his dream of representing his new country at the Olympics a reality. In the meantime, he needed to get a job. A few days after arriving in Israel, Misha was standing on his balcony when a man came up and asked him if he wanted to work. Misha said yes, and found himself hauling cement bags on a construction site in the broiling Middle East sun. By the end of the day he'd suffered heatstroke, and came to the realization that it was time to get back to the cooler atmosphere where he belonged.

He contacted Yossi Goldberg, mayor of Metulla, the location of Israel's only ice rink. Yossi assured Misha that his facility was regulation-size and invited him to come north for a look. When he

AFTER BEATING THE ODDS AND REPRESENTING ISRAEL AT THE 1998 OLYMPICS, MISHA SHMERKIN FOUND HIMSELF SITTING OUT THE 1998–1999 SEASON THANKS TO HIS EX-WIFE. SARIT SHMERKIN CLAIMED MISHA WAS NOT PAYING HER APPROPRIATE ALIMONY OR CHILD SUPPORT FOR THEIR SON, ADI, AND SO RECEIVED A COURT ORDER FORBIDDING HIM TO LEAVE THE COUNTRY.

federation head Yossi Goldberg convinced him that, as an ambassador of Israel, now was the time to stand tall and show the world what he could do.

Misha stepped out on the ice wearing a skullcap and asked for a moment of silence in Rabin's memory. He then went on to skate the performance of his life and win the silver medal. He did what he'd been urged to do. To the best of his ability, he represented Israel—the country that accepted him when no one else would.

Switzerland's Lucinda Ruh also knows the misery of skating in a nation that makes it clear it doesn't want her.

Born in Zurich, Lucinda was four when her father's job moved them to Japan. She began skating at age six, and by age eight, was taking lessons from Nabuo Sato, who'd coached his daughter, Yuka, to the 1994 World Championship. Despite speaking fluent Japanese (as well as German, French, and English), Lucinda felt like an outsider. Other skaters at the rink weren't happy to see a blonde, blue-eyed European girl taking up ice and lesson time they believed to be rightfully theirs, and they made certain Lucinda was aware of their displeasure.

America's Tonia Kwiatkowski faced a different obstacle. It wasn't that her country didn't think she belonged there—people simply thought she was too old to still be competing. After all, in an age of fourteen-year-old world champions, shouldn't Tonia be thinking about retirement? Heading into the 1998 Olympic season, she was a month short of her twenty-seventh (!) birthday. (She ended up placing fourth at the 1998 Nationals, missing the Olympics by one spot, though she did compete at the 1998 Worlds.)

The question of age had been dogging Tonia since she passed her teen years. At twenty-five, at the 1996 Nationals, the good-humored skater appeared at a press conference hobbling on a walker. Dismissed as the perennial also-ran, Tonia won the silver that year and earned a spot on the World Team. She claims, "I think of myself as the Cal Ripkin of skating. I keep coming back and giving you more."

got there, Misha found a rink half the size of an Olympic one, with a host of self-proclaimed experts who tried to convince him that it was actually bigger than it looked.

With the help of the Canadian Jewish community, a regulation-size rink was finally built in Metulla. Misha trained there for the 1994 Olympics and for 1995 Skate Canada, the site of his greatest victory and his greatest personal challenge.

Hours before he was set to skate the long program, a fellow skater ran up to Misha and told him, "Your president's been shot." Prime Minister Yitzhak Rabin's assassination sent shock waves around the world, leaving a stunned Misha to cry, "I never thought a Jew could lift his hand against another Jew." He considered withdrawing from the competition, but

POLITICS

Five-time Russian ladies' champion and 1998 European champion Maria Butyrskaya is convinced that the Russian Skating Federation is against her. She claims that after the 1993 Worlds, where she failed to qualify for the final and lost Russia its only chance to send a woman to the 1994 Olympics, the federation decided that she was finished and did everything in their power to ensure she got the message and quit. The federation allegedly tried to keep her from winning the 1996 Russian title by pulling their darling, 1994 European bronze medalist Olga Markova, "up by the ears," in Maria's words, to try and keep her in first place. Olga's disastrous performance made that impossible, and the title went to Maria. Still, the federation refused to automatically name Maria to the World Team, telling her that they would wait for the results of the Europeans (Maria finished third, Olga eleventh) and the results of the Centennial Competition (Maria finished second, ahead of Michelle Kwan) to make up their minds. Until a week before the 1996 World Championship, Maria didn't know if she would be allowed to go. Once there, she finished fourth.

Her problems continued into the 1997 season. Maria claims that the federation didn't send her to Continent's Cup because they didn't want her earning the prize money there. She claims that the Russian Nationals are always her toughest competition. Unlike the international stage where the judges like her. It's back home where she is made to feel like an interloper on the team.

Such claims would be easier to discount if they were issued from only one somewhat embittered young woman (when queried about her teammate, Irina Slutskaya, who at the age of sixteen, in 1996, became the first Russian woman to win the European Championship, Maria sniped, "Of course, everything is easy when you are sixteen. Just wait for her to grow and try to do the same with a woman's body"). However, the 1996 world pair champions Marina Eltsova and Andrei Bushkov repeat Maria's charges. First, they believe that their 1994 Olympic prospect was stolen from them by the returning professionals, Gordeeva and Grinkov and Mishkutenok and Dmitriev. They claim that their coach, Igor Moskvin, was more interested and invested in helping his wife, Tamara Moskvina, with her team, Mishkutenok and Dmitriev, than in training his own, and that the Russian Skating Federation, even before the Nationals, had already decided to send the reinstated pros to the Olympics to reap the publicity value of it.

Despite Eltsova and Bushkov's winning the 1995 Nationals, Moskvin told them it was time to quit eligible skating. Tamara suggested they become professionals, and the team did briefly join an ice show, before deciding to give the eligible scene one more try—this time with a coach who was actually supportive of them. They switched to a new coach and a new choreographer and won the World Championship in 1996. But Marina and Andrei's problems with the federation weren't over.

Like Maria, they believe they aren't the political favorites of the federation, and that president Valentin Piseev would prefer another team to represent Russia. In addition, though Marina and Andrei receive only 200,000 rubles (about $45) a month from the Olympic Committee to defray their training expenses, they claim that the federation is hindering their earning extra income by limiting the number of shows and Pro/Ams they can appear in.

The federation's position is that too many shows and Pro/Ams tire their athletes out for the important eligible competitions. Says coach Alexei Mishin, "You can work to make a champion, or you can work to make money." But a great many Russian skaters often disobey direct orders to stay home and accept invitations to skate in Western exhibitions, hoping that federation president Piseev won't find out.

However, it isn't only the Russian Skating Federation that encounters complaints and accusations of unfairness from its skaters. Philippe Candeloro, 1994 world silver medalist, found himself in similiar circumstances when he flew from France to the United States to appear in the CBS special *Too Hot to Skate II*. Only after he arrived did Candelero find out the French Skating Federation had denied him approval to skate on the same ice as professionals like Oksana Baiul and Scott Hamilton. The federation threatened to cancel his Olympic eligibil-

ity if he performed, so a furious Philippe boarded a plane and returned home.

The following season, the federation would face an even bigger crisis. In July 1997, they declared bankruptcy to freeze their $8.1 million debt until October. Suddenly, it looked like France's skaters, who turned to the federation to cover their training and travel expenses, might have to look elsewhere for their funds. Adding insult to injury, prize money won by French skaters and given to the federation for eventual distribution was frozen along with the other assets, meaning that skaters couldn't even count on the money they had personally earned. Pascal Lavanchy told *International Figure Skating* in December 1997, "If this situation continues, France will be ousted [from the Olympics] by the year 2002."

In the meantime, the USFSA has dealt with its own share of censure about a federation playing politics with skaters' lives.

At the 1994 Nationals, more than one eyebrow was raised when the pair team of Karen Courtland and Todd Reynolds, in spite of three huge falls in their long program, was given an Olympic berth over Kuchiki and Marvel, who skated with no major errors. The crowd booed their marks, and a letter to the March 1994 *American Skating World* accused, "This competition was not judged on what was put on the ice that day. This event was prejudged, the Olympic team picked before anyone skated."

It was an old accusation, one that had been leveled against both the USFSA and the ISU. In the past, compulsory figures were the great equalizer. Remembers Jirina Ribbens, "They could either push you or hold you back any which way they wanted [with figures]. Certain people like Robin Cousins and Denise Biellmann were held back until they were ready for them, then, all of a sudden, they had good figures. It was, like, a miracle! But Gary Beacom, who had excellent figures, never got any marks for them. And Toller Cranston, too." If they weren't spectacular in freestyle, skaters could be buried so low in the figures that there was no chance of them pulling a Trixie Schuba into a medal, and risk confounding the television audience.

In 1996, another controversy erupted when defending national champion and world bronze medalist Nicole Bobek, who had to pull out of the U.S. Championship because of an ankle injury, was denied a bye to the 1996 World Championship. There was no precedent for such a refusal. Two years earlier, an injured Nancy Kerrigan was named to the Olympic team based merely on her being the previous year's U.S. champion. She wasn't even a defending world medalist like Nicole. In 1992,

MANY BELIEVED THAT
KAREN COURTLAND
AND TODD REYNOLDS
DIDN'T DESERVE TO
BE AT THE 1994
OLYMPICS.
COURTLAND AND
REYNOLDS TRIPPED
ALL OVER THEM-
SELVES AT THE U.S.
NATIONALS, YET
STILL RECEIVED
SCORES HIGH
ENOUGH TO PLACE
THEM ON THE
OLYMPIC TEAM.

a hurt Todd Eldredge was also given a bye to the Olympics. ABC announcer Dick Button was so certain Nicole would receive her bye that he went off the air for the night predicting it. Yet the USFSA said no. They never offered a concrete reason why, although speculation ran that the USFSA had decided to punish Nicole for the manner in which she received her injury.

Instead of training for Nationals, Nicole accepted $90,000 to appear (along with Todd Eldredge) in a tour of *Nutcracker on Ice*—one of the financial perks available to the new eligible skaters. The USFSA, agreeing with Russian federation head Piseev, believed their athletes should be home practicing, not on the road padding their bank accounts. They decided to send their message, loud and clear, courtesy of Nicole. That same year, Nicole's *Nutcracker* costar, Todd Eldredge, lost his U.S. title to Rudy Galindo. In the weeks between Nationals and

Worlds, reneging on a reported $100,000 worth of exhibition commitments, Todd stayed home and trained. He won the 1996 World Championship. Message received.

COUNTRY-HOPPING

While powerhouse countries like the U.S., Russia, and France always have more deserving skaters than they have slots for on their World and Olympic teams, many smaller countries have to scramble just to field a single adequate entry. As a result, good skaters who regularly find themselves just barely missing a spot on their own nation's podium periodically decide to finesse their way into international competition, and begin desperately searching for another site in which to hitch their star.

American-born Dianne DeLeeuw won the 1975 World Championship representing her mother's homeland, the Netherlands. Before she became the 1997 U.S. pair champion with her partner, Jason Dungjen, Tokyo-born Kyoko Ina finished fourth as a single at the 1987 Japanese Nationals, though she confesses, "I felt like an outsider. I grew up in America and to go to another country to compete didn't feel right." Alice Sue Clayes, 1990 U.S. junior champion, decided there was too much competition at the senior level and began skating for Belgium, qualifying because one of her grandparents had been born there. Todd Sand, 1996 U.S. pair champion, once represented Denmark.

Canadians Isabelle and Paul Duchesnay became the 1991 world ice dance champions skating under the French flag. Their countrymen, Allison MacLean and Konrad Schaub, represented Austria at the 1996 Worlds. Through a series of bureaucratic gyrations, Tokyo-born, one-time U.S. competitor Kaho Kainuma managed to

IN 1996, RUDY GALINDO BECAME THE OLDEST MAN TO WIN THE U.S. CHAMPIONSHIP IN THIRTY-TWO YEARS. HIS UPSET VICTORY INSPIRED NUMEROUS SKATERS—AMONG THEM MICHAEL CHACK, SHEPHERD CLARK, DAN HOLLANDER, DAMON ALLEN, AND JOHN BALDWIN, JR.—TO POSTPONE RETIREMENT AND KEEP COMPETING IN THE HOPES OF "PULLING A RUDY."

get on the 1997 Armenian team, where her primary competition for the spot came from Jennifer Goolsbee, an American who'd once surrendered her citizenship to represent Germany. But that wasn't the end of Jennifer.

After finishing ninth at the 1994 Olympics with German partner Hendryk Schamberger, Jennifer gave up her German citizenship when Hendryk retired from skating to go to medical school. She then paired up with Samuel Gezalian, son of a Jewish mother and an Armenian father, who won Skate America '91 representing the U.S.S.R. Samuel turned down a chance to skate for Israel in order to take advantage of the Byelorussian citizenship of his partner, Tatiana Navka, and then, when that partnership broke up, teamed up with Jennifer. They won the 1997 German Nationals, but she no longer held the citizenship necessary to represent the country at Worlds. Jennifer reapplied for her citizenship, but the German government, fed up with her capriciousness, refused. Jennifer and Samuel then promptly decided to turn Armenian in time for the Olympics, but the Armenians weren't buying either.

For skaters from the former U.S.S.R. eager to try the same trick, the collapse of the Soviet Union offered a host of new republics to choose from. Russian Igor Pashkevitch declared himself a citizen of Azerbaijan, as did the equally ethnic Russian Yulia Vorobieva. If no republic was available, a neighboring nation would do. Moscow's Julia Lautowa moved to Austria with her coach, lived in Vienna just long enough to acquire her citizenship and win the Austrian title, then returned home and continued to train in Moscow while representing Austria. Andrei Vlachtchenko, a Ukrainian born in Germany while his father served there with the occupying Soviet army, first represented the U.S.S.R., then his mother's home, Latvia, before seeking German citizenship in 1994. He represented Germany at the 1996 and 1997 Worlds and was looking forward to the 1998 Olympics when a second drunk-driving conviction (the first came in 1995) stripped him of his German passport.

CHANGING THE RULES

Brian Boitano, 1988 Olympic champion, wanted to go to the 1994 Olympics—a prospect that seemed permanently closed to him as a result of his turning pro, competing in pro events, and starring in his own television special. Brian argued in the June 1993 issue of *Skating* magazine, "Skating should be inclusive. You should be able to do competitions, shows, and television work. I don't see why pro competitions are the only ones I can do." He lobbied the ISU for a change in the rules that would allow professionals to take part in any activity they wanted to. "Sooner or later," he predicted, "everybody's going to be equal."

As a result of Brian's efforts, for the 1994 Olympics, pro skaters were given a chance to, in the words of one insider, "get their virginity back." They could be reinstated and, like the eligible skaters, try for a spot on their respective Olympic teams.

Like Boitano, 1984 and 1988 Olympic champion Katarina Witt, 1988 Olympic bronze medalist and 1992 Olympic champion Viktor Petrenko, 1988 Olympic pair champions Gordeeva and Grinkov, 1992 Olympic pair champions Mishkutenok and Dmitriev, and 1984 Olympic dance champions Torvill and Dean chose to return to Olympic ice.

It was not a popular decision among the former "amateurs," many of whom believed that those who'd already won medals should step aside and give someone else a chance at glory. After all, the pros had nothing to gain by another win—they were already major stars and already commanded very substantial appearance fees.

On the other hand, eligible skaters had everything to lose.

Without an Olympic medal, they could never hope to reach the heights of Boitano, Witt, or Torvill and Dean. Skaters like 1992 U.S. bronze medalist Mark Mitchell felt they were being robbed of their opportunity by pros who'd already taken advantage of theirs. Boitano argued, "Because of what we're doing now, Mark Mitchell is going to be able to compete forever. Doors will be open for years to come."

One reinstated skater who didn't receive nearly the publicity of her counterparts was 1982 world champion Elaine Zayak. The one-time triple-jump teen wonder had retired from competitive skating in 1984, but watching Nationals on television nine years later prompted her to assess the ladies' field and think, "I can do that."

She began to train again, using the blades she'd broken in at the 1984 Olympics. She lost twenty pounds (9kg). She relearned her triples. In her first reinstated competition, she finished thirteenth, behind girls who couldn't yet walk— forget skate—when Elaine won the Worlds almost a decade earlier.

Yet finishing second at the eastern sectional qualified Elaine for Nationals. Once there, no one gave her a thought. After all, the field was jammed with jumping-bean teenagers, and Elaine, at twenty-eight, was even older than Tonia Kwiatkowski!

But when the teenagers began falling, the more seasoned Elaine remained on her feet. She finished fourth overall, winning the pewter medal and standing on the podium with Tonya Harding, Michelle Kwan, and Nicole Bobek. Elaine missed making the Olympic team by just two places, but the Olympis was never the point. "Nationals was my goal," she says. "All I wanted to prove was that I could skate as well as I had ever skated. And I did."

Which was more than could be said for the pre-event favorite, Brian Boitano. A slight toe catch on the triple lutz and a singled triple axel put him in second place behind defending champion Scott Davis—a decision that proved quite popular in the skater-seating section of the arena, packed as it was with eligible skaters, none of whom had greeted news that their spots on the U.S. international team might be filled with returning pros too kindly.

The bad feeling directed at returning pros continued at the Olympics. A crash in his short program left Boitano sixth overall, Petrenko fourth, Witt seventh, Torvill and Dean third, and Mishkutenok and Dmitriev second. Only Gordeeva and Grinkov regained the gold. But after the Olympics every single one of them—without even a perfunctory stop at the Worlds to help their countries qualify for next year's championship—returned to the professional ranks and their six-figure appearance fees. The new rules gave them the best of both worlds.

Now that professionals had gotten a chance to play at being amateurs again, it wasn't long before the amateurs won their right to be treated as professionals, and the stakes for winning a national, a world, and an Olympic title grew even higher.

In the end, the changes made skating more worthwhile, justifying the parental sacrifices, the expenses, the injuries, the merry-go-round of partners, the personal and political battles, the country-hopping, and, when all else fails, lobbying for changes in the rules. With so much at stake, most skaters today would do anything to get to the top.

THE RETURN OF THE PROFESSIONALS TO AMATEUR SKATING IN 1994 DROVE 1992 U.S. BRONZE MEDALIST MARK MITCHELL (LEFT WITH KURT BROWNING AND SCOTT HAMILTON) OUT OF THE SPORT, AND INTO—IRONICALLY—PROFESSIONAL COMPETITION.

PROFESSIONAL COMPETITION

FOR SOME, PROFESSIONAL SKATING IS A MEANS TO FURTHER GLORY AND FAME. FOR OTHERS,
LIKE CHINA'S CHEN LU AND UKRAINE'S VIKTOR PETRENKO, THE CHANCE TO EARN MONEY
BY COMPETING OFFERS A WAY OUT OF POVERTY.

In 1952, when Dick Button won his second Olympic gold medal and turned professional, he wanted to keep competing, but there was no place for him to go to fulfill that ambition. Even a decade later, the only professional competitive opportunity was the World Professional Competition in Jaca, Spain. (Established in England in 1931, it moved to Spain in the 1960s.) However, that event, which was mostly for ice show skaters, was an "open" contest that accepted all comers regardless of ability. The majority performed the same numbers they skated every night in shows like Ice Capades, only without show-lighting, and were judged by their peers. Prize money was $2,500 for singles and $3,000 to be split between both partners in a pairs or dance team.

After convincing ABC and CBS to televise amateur events, Button approached the ISU in the late 1960s with a plan to start a similar professional circuit, but interest was minimal. The ISU thought a pro world championship was too radical an idea.

A NEW PROFESSIONAL SPORT

Working independently in 1973, Button presented the initial World Professional Figure Skating Championship in Tokyo. His plan was to provide a place where skaters could develop their craft and artistry, a sort of graduate school for the elite. He wanted to give every skater the opportunity to keep growing as a performer and a technician, and to this day, he is disappointed when some fail to take advantage of their chance or when he sees pro skaters who don't change or progress from who they were as amateurs. Petr Barna, 1992 Olympic bronze medalist, used to drive Button crazy. Button wanted to know why no one would take Barna in hand and do something with him, teach him to stand up, to stretch, to have a concept for a routine. It broke Button's heart, because he saw wasted potential.

Button also wanted to establish a pro competition as a setting for skaters to earn sufficient money. In 1973, first prize at the World Professional

Championship was $15,000 in each category. (The prize money in all four disciplines currently stands at $40,000 for first place, $20,000 for second, $12,000 for third, and $8,000 for fourth. Those sums are modest compared to the appearance fees commanded by most big-name skaters, regardless of final placement. Dorothy Hamill, in her prime, skated for no less than $100,000 a night; Kristi Yamaguchi regularly earns up to $250,000.)

The first competitors at the event included the newly turned pro Janet Lynn beating Hungary's Zsuzsa Almassy. As an indicator of the upsets that were soon to characterize professional competition, the last time Lynn and Almassy had gone head-to-head, at the 1969 Worlds, Janet finished fifth while Almassy won the bronze. In the men's division, American spinning sensation and 1955 and 1956 world silver medalist Ronnie Robertson defeated Canada's Don Jackson, the 1962 world champion and the first man to perform a triple lutz in competition. In last place was John Misha Petkevich, who won his only U.S. title in 1971, fifteen years after Robertson retired.

The pairs division was won by the Soviet Olympic champs, the Protopopovs. Determined that his World Professional Championship would live up to the internationalism of its name, Button invited them through the Russian Skating Federation. The skaters were dying to come, but until the moment they stepped off the plane in Japan, no one knew whether their government would let them. (Because the federation refused to cooperate, the next Soviets to compete at World Pros were 1984 Olympic and 1988 world champions Valova and Vasiliev in 1989. When Button's Candid Productions tried to request Soviet skaters through official channels, they were always turned down. It was only when Button's people went straight to the skaters themselves that Russians became World Pro regulars.)

As unwilling to give up control in the 1970s as they would be in the 1990s, the ISU fought Button's "unauthorized" championship, making it necessary to wait seven years before another one could be

held. (In the meantime, Button put on events called World Skate Challenges to bypass the ISU's objections over his use of the words "world championship.")

Following the 1980 Olympics, Button attempted to put together an event pitting established stars like Peggy Fleming and Dorothy Hamill against "kids" fresh from the Olympics. However, the older skaters were afraid that losing a professional event would somehow diminish their Olympic titles. The only way Button could convince them to take part was to make the 1980 World Pro a team competition with no individual scores.

That first contest proved so successful—despite the "Stars of the 1980 Olympics" team, including Games silver medalist Linda Fratianne, gold medalist Robin Cousins, bronze medalist Charlie Tickner, and Babilonia and Gardner, soundly defeating the "World and Olympic Professional Stars" team of Fleming, Hamill, and Starbuck and Shelley—that their team format stayed in place through 1981 and 1982. In 1983, for the first time, individual results for all four divisions were tallied in addition to the

team event, though prize money still went to the top team. That year, Janet Lynn prevailed over Dorothy Hamill, who in their last head-to-head had finished fourth to Janet's second at the 1973 Worlds, as well as over Linda Fratianne who, back in 1973, at age twelve, was only the U.S. junior silver medalist.

However, in the men's contest, youth prevailed as 1980 Olympic bronze medalist Charlie Tickner beat 1976 Olympic bronze medalist Toller Cranston and 1960 Olympic bronze medalist Don Jackson.

ABC's Wilson says, "Dick Button was a pioneer in many respects, and he was a pioneer in giving skaters a venue where they could compete for money and earn a living outside of skating in shows. He's now created, in a sense, his own league."

Candid Productions vice president Jirina Ribbens credits the success of those first World Pros as well as the subsequent ones to "a combination of sponsor, television, and public. You can't have [pro competitions] just for the public. It doesn't pay for itself. The production costs are way out there."

Viewers at home never saw the competition in the same order as the fans who watched it live, because of the preferences of the television audiences. Explains Ribbens, "It's very ironic that, for the public at large, skating is all about women. For skating fans, skating is all about men. When you do an event live, you always have to end with the men if you want the best evening. When you do an event for television, you always want to end with the women, if you want people to stay tuned. If we play the competition the way it runs live [with men as the final event], we lose viewers. But if you keep teasing the women, TV viewers will stay tuned."

The year 1984 brought a bumper crop of new professionals, with Olympic champions Torvill and Dean, 1984 world champions Underhill and Martini, and Olympic gold medalist Scott Hamilton winning their categories. Only 1984 Olympic silver medalist Rosalynn Sumners, perhaps failing to grasp the contrast between amateur and pro competition, finished fourth in the ladies', behind winner Dorothy Hamill, longtime rival and 1982 world champion Elaine Zayak, and Fratianne.

In 1985, the growing success of the World Pros prompted ABC to ask Dick Button and Candid Productions for another event, one that would take place outside the United States. So the Challenge of Champions debuted in France. Unlike the World Pro, which features technical and artistic programs (with two sets of scores for each) for men, ladies, and pairs, and a rhythm dance and free dance for the ice dancers, the Challenge of Champions presented a single program, judged both artistically and technically, followed by an exhibition gala the same evening.

The year 1985 was also the last in which World Pros would be scored as a team event, though individual scores were again noted. Dorothy Hamill along with Torvill and Dean won their second consecutive pro titles, and Babilonia and Gardner finally broke free from last place, where they'd languished in 1983 and 1984. They won the pairs title over the Protopopovs, who had retired from amateur skating in 1969, two years before Tai and Randy entered their first novice competition. Among the men, fans

TAI BABILONIA AND RANDY GARDNER EARNED THEIR NICKNAME, "THE HEARTBREAK KIDS," AFTER RANDY'S GROIN INJURY FORCED THEM TO WITHDRAW FROM THE 1980 OLYMPICS. AS DEFENDING WORLD CHAMPIONS, THEY MIGHT HAVE BEEN FAVORED TO WIN THE GOLD—EXCEPT THAT THEY'D WON THEIR TITLE DURING A YEAR WHEN 1976 OLYMPIC CHAMPIONS IRINA RODNINA AND ALEXANDER ZAITSEV (AGAINST WHOM BABILONIA AND GARDNER HAD ONLY EARNED A BRONZE AT THE 1978 WORLDS) DECLINED TO COMPETE. IN THE LONG RUN, WITHDRAWING MAY HAVE BROUGHT THE PAIR MORE FAME AND RECOGNITION THAN THE INEVITABLE DISAPPOINTMENT THAT WOULD HAVE FOLLOWED ANY OLYMPIC MEDAL LESS THAN THE MEDIA-HYPED GOLD.

got their first look at the rivalry that would dominate the next two years of World Pros. Robin Cousins, 1980 Olympic champion, performing a classic soft-shoe, defeated the 1984 champion, Scott Hamilton. He repeated that feat at the inaugural Challenge of Champions. A year later, the standings would flip as Hamilton's emotional "Battle Hymn of the Republic," in memory of the 1961 U.S. team killed in a plane crash, outscored Cousins' more modern, electric-music exhibition. Hamilton would also go on to win the Challenge of Champions.

However, in 1987, judges preferred Cousins' equally modern "Machinery" over Hamilton's comic forecast of "When I'm 64." Comments Ribbens, "Robin changed day and night when he became a pro. He started to work with artists, he started working on concepts, he started to think. He transformed himself....[Without pro competitions] he wouldn't have had the opportunity. In a show, why would he have challenged himself? When Robin came to World Pro in 1980, he worked with people like Peggy Fleming, and he saw that there was more

pitting gold medalist Boitano against silver medalist and 1987 world champion Brian Orser. Unfortunately, Orser didn't so much dazzle as confound the judges, coming out in Indian war paint with tufts of hay strapped to his arm and leg to perform "The Lion Sleeps Tonight." The hay made it difficult for Orser to control his jumps, and the decline in technique of the first man to do two triple axels in a program allowed for Scott Hamilton, who'd barely been mentioned in the pre-event hoopla, to skate a high-energy, jump-packed, dazzling gold-lamé "In the Mood," thereby vaulting into second place behind Boitano, whose technical level, triple axel and all, had not dropped a notch since the Olympics.

Traditionally, each new influx of post-Olympic skaters raised the level of pro competition. Having top-level skaters compete head-to-head raised the bar and led to exciting matches and performances for fans. Remembers Ribbens, "Starting in the mid-'80s, when World Pro went from team competition to an individual competition, that got everybody's pride going. It was competitive between Robin and Scott, so it pushed them to keep their level up. But when Boitano came in, that's when it went up to the next level. He brought his technical skills. He didn't scale down from what he did at the Olympics. And that pushed everybody. Next year [post-1998 Olympics] we expect more. I don't expect Elvis [Stojko] to do less than a quad in his program."

to skating than just doing your tricks. It must have opened his eyes, because, by the time the individual competitions came around, he was ready for them."

The year 1988 was another Olympic year, meaning new blood for the World Pros. In pairs and dance, respectively, Olympic bronze medalists Jill Watson and Peter Oppegard and Tracy Wilson and Robert McCall could finish no higher than last. Ladies' bronze medalist Debi Thomas had better luck, winning the event and halting Hamill's four-year winning streak. In spite of winning three World Pro titles (in 1988, 1989, and 1991), Thomas gave up the circuit, returned to medical school, and, in 1997, graduated from Northwestern University a month before giving birth to her first child.

The 1988 World Pro men's event was trumpeted as a rematch of Calgary's "Battle of the Brians"—

TWO-TIME OLYMPIC SILVER MEDALIST BRIAN ORSER HIT THE NEWS AGAIN IN 1998, WHEN, TEN YEARS AFTER THE "BATTLE OF THE BRIANS," HE FAILED TO KEEP AN EX-BOYFRIEND'S PALIMONY SUIT FROM GOING PUBLIC. DESPITE BRIAN'S STATED FEARS THAT REVELATION OF HIS HOMOSEXUALITY WOULD HURT HIS PUBLIC IMAGE, FANS IN CANADA AND THE U.S. PROVED VERY SUPPORTIVE, AND HIS ON-ICE POPULARITY, IN FACT, SOARED.

Boitano would continue to win from 1989 to 1992. After skipping 1993, he returned to finish first in 1994. He would also win the Challenge of Champions from 1988 to 1991. Orser, conversely, slipped to last place in 1989, behind not only Boitano and Hamilton but also Gary Beacom. Despite never winning a world or Olympic medal, the idiosyncratic Beacom—he has performed wearing skates on his hands and wrapped from head to toe in black nylon—proved rather popular on the pro circuit, where his penchant for oddness was admired rather than shunned.

The other 1989 upset came in ice dance. Wilson and McCall finally defeated Russia's Bestemianova and Bukin, the Soviet Olympic champions whom they never once succeeded in dethroning as amateurs. Like Beacom, Bestemianova and Bukin took advantage of turning pro by going wild. Among their esoteric, often abstract routines was a tribute to victims of the Armenian earthquake, during which Bukin appeared to die four times; an exploration of the Russian soul with both portraying the "mad monk" Rasputin; and a living reenactment of a Russian parable "A fish may fall in love with a bird, but where would they live?" Unlike Beacom, however, Bestemianova and Bukin's profound artistic vision most often caused the judges and the public to quizzically scratch their heads. Despite participating in four World Pros, they only managed to win one, in 1991.

They did, however, win the 1989 Challenge of Champions, held for the first time in Moscow. In second place behind them was another Russian couple, Natalia Annenko and Genrikh Sretenski, the epitome of a team whose greatest success came in the professional ranks. Second at the 1988 Europeans and fourth at the 1988 Olympics, Annenko and Sretenski had never won a world or Olympic medal.

They retired from amateur competition in 1988, a year after their coach, Ludmilla Pakhomova, died, and assumed their skating days were over. A pro career seemed out of the question. They weren't well known enough to challenge for spots with a show or tour. Yet, that first invitation to compete at the Moscow Challenge of Champions proved better than a gold medal, as their placing there led to a slot at the World Pro, which, after two more second places, they finally won in 1992 and 1993. The latter year, the team came out on top over brand-new Olympic gold medalists Klimova and Ponomarenko, who never managed to win a World Pro. That team finished second in 1995 and 1996 before taking a break from competition due to Klimova's pregnancy (she gave birth to a boy, Timothy, in February 1998, almost exactly six years to the day after winning Olympic gold).

In 1990, it was time for Klimova and Ponomarenko's countrymen, Ekaterina Gordeeva and Sergei Grinkov, to discover that even four world titles and an Olympic gold do not guarantee victory among the pros. Skating to the classical "Scheherazade," they finished second behind five-time World Pro champions Barbara Underhill and Paul Martini, who made up for a lack of technical perfection with a crowd-pleasing popular style. Their "When a Man Loves a Woman" routine, performed with Martini in torn jeans and Underhill in a slip, is still considered by many to be the hottest seduction ever put on the ice. Praises Ribbens, "They used the World Pros to change their skating. They were very limited because he couldn't jump, but they made sure they did what they could do very, very well. The package was right."

Another 1990 surprise came in the form of Switzerland's Denise Biellmann. The first woman to complete a triple lutz and the 1981 world champion, she was none the less considered too passé to be much of a factor at the World Pros. Yet her win over Sumners, Thomas, and 1988 Olympic silver medalist Elizabeth Manley ushered in a new phase of Denise's career—where her professional titles eclipsed her achievements as an amateur.

Ribbens believes, "Denise was young when she left amateurs so she didn't develop into the great skater she could be until she was already a pro."

OLYMPIC CHAMPIONS
TRADITIONALLY TEND
TO REPEAT THEIR
VICTORY AT THE
SAME YEAR'S WORLD
CHAMPIONSHIPS.
KRISTI YAMAGUCHI
(ABOVE) WON THE
1992 OLYMPICS AND
THE 1992 WORLDS.
IN 1994, HOWEVER,
NONE OF THE LADIES
OF LILLEHAMMER—
OKSANA BAIUL
(GOLD), NANCY
KERRIGAN (SILVER),
OR LU CHEN
(BRONZE)—CHOSE TO
ATTEND THE WORLD
CHAMPIONSHIP IN
JAPAN, LEAVING THE
DOOR OPEN FOR YUKA
SATO (RIGHT) TO WIN
THE TITLE IN HER
HOME COUNTRY.

With the proliferation of pro competitions in the 1990s, Denise, whose repertoire continues to pack more triple jumps than many men on the circuit, would win the 1992, 1994, 1995, and 1996 Miko Masters, the 1994 American Invitational, and the 1996 Masters on Ice. The experience and confidence she gained from winning those smaller pro competitions helped Denise finish second in 1997 at the more competitive U.S. Pros, ahead of 1994 Olympic silver medalist Nancy Kerrigan, and win the Challenge of Champions over 1992 Olympic gold medalist Kristi Yamaguchi.

As Boitano did for the men in 1988, Kristi raised the technical stakes of ladies' competition with her post-Olympic entry into the pro ranks. Triple jumps won Kristi the 1992 World Pro and Challenge of Champions. But in 1993, even she had to get in line behind the 1989 world champion from Japan, Midori Ito, who came to World Pro competition with a weapon no other woman could boast—a triple axel. In 1994, Kristi's superior artistry held off not only Midori Ito, but the 1994 world champion from Japan, Yuka Sato. Unlike her predecessors, who'd had four years to reign as Olympic champion, a scheduling quirk wherein the Winter Games were shifted two years ahead to keep them from falling in the same year as the Summer Games (a move prompted in part by television's desire to have a big sporting event to sell advertising for more often) gave Kristi only two years of unchallenged glory. (Those who believe that Kristi's Japanese heritage kept her from attaining the America's-sweetheart heights achieved by previous Olympic champs Fleming and Hamill can presumably add the Olympic shift to their conspiracy theory.)

Another American suffering from that too-short fate was 1992 Olympic silver medalist Paul Wylie. Never a national champion or world medalist, Wylie skated the performance of his life in France to finish second behind the Ukraine's Viktor Petrenko. When he moved into the pros, his future seemed splendid. However, the inconsistency that prevented Wylie from winning major titles as an amateur continued to plague him as a

ALTHOUGH MOST
SKATERS TEND TO
FORGO HIGHER
EDUCATION, THE
ONES WHO DO DECIDE
TO PURSUE IT AT
THE ELITE LEVEL
HISTORICALLY END
UP AT HARVARD.
TWO-TIME OLYMPIC
CHAMPION DICK
BUTTON IS A
GRADUATE, AS ARE
1956 OLYMPIC
CHAMPION TENLEY
ALBRIGHT, 1969
U.S. CHAMPION JOHN
MISHA PETKEVICH,
AND 1992 OLYMPIC
SILVER MEDALIST
PAUL WYLIE (LEFT).

pro. When he was good, he was very, very good, beating Boitano, Orser, and Petrenko in 1992 to win the Challenge of Champions. But when he was bad, Paul could disintegrate faster than practically any other skater. His programs were works of art, high concepts including "Schindler's List," "Henry V," "Bring Him Home," "The Untouchables," "Carmina Burana," and "Mission: Impossible." They were also all disturbingly identical, to the point that it began to seem as if he were skating the same number to a different piece of music every year. Each began with a spiral into the triple flip, and featured similar hand gestures and tortured facial expressions. Though he won the World Pro in 1993, Paul finished second in 1992 and 1994, and last in both 1995 and 1996. He was invited to the 1997 event, but declined the invitation. Having just won the 1997 Challenge, he chose to finish his professional career on a positive note.

The man who beat Wylie out for the gold in Albertville, Viktor Petrenko, also has been accused of suffering from the similarity syndrome. Viktor's programs fall into two categories. First, there are those skated to classical music, where much time is spent on conveying abstract concepts through desperate arm waving and a tortured expression to rival Wylie's. And then there are Viktor's hip-hop numbers. Usually performed to rap or rock and roll, these crowd-pleasing programs highlight Viktor's showmanship—he spends most of his time standing still and gyrating his hips while a chorus of teenage fans squeals approvingly in the background.

Those squeals were clearly echoed by the television audience, as ratings for World Pros continued to grow every year. In 1990, the show moved from its weekend afternoon broadcast slot to a prime-time, hour-long special. In 1992, it expanded to two hours in prime time, picking up four million more viewers along the way. In 1993, the competition attracted three million more. In 1994, with skating interest still post-Olympic hot, the World Pros captured an average of 20 percent of the entire viewing audience.

That same year, two-time Olympic champions Gordeeva and Grinkov turned pro for the second time in their career and won the pairs event (their third World Pro title). Usova and Zhulin, 1994 Olympic silver medalists, won the dance, while Boitano won the men's—coming out ahead of Wylie, Hamilton, and four-time world champion Kurt Browning, the Canadian whose passage to a pro career proved rockier than most.

Browning finished third at the 1994 Challenge of Champions and fourth at the 1995 Challenge behind Robin Cousins, who, courtesy of a bad back and knees, had long given up triple jumps. It was a rather poor showing for a recent world champion. What made Browing's situation more unusual than Wylie's was that, except for coming into both the 1992 and 1994 Olympics as the favorite and leaving without a medal each time, Kurt made his reputation as the king of consistency and as the first man to land a quadruple jump in competition. For him to fail to win a major pro title his first year out was a surprise to his fans.

It wasn't until Kurt the brilliant jumper became Kurt the artist that his fortunes began to change. Says Ribbens, "Skaters who come to World Pro keep their technical level, and they develop as artists. Our focus is on great technical skating in all aspects of skating. In body positions, spirals, spins, jumps. And to be a great entertainer. Because what good is it if you can do beautiful jumps, but you can't keep the audience's interest?"

Once Kurt Browning understood and mastered that formula, things began to change. He went on to win the World Pro in 1995, 1996, and 1997, and established himself as one of the sport's most popular men. Ribbens believes he has the potential to go even further in the future, revealing, "He has an incredible routine to 'Romeo and Juliet.' It's music from the fighting scenes. His wife choreographed it, with lots of ballet steps. But it's so difficult, he's only done it in competition once. I begged him to do it at the World Pro. But it's a very intense routine, and he isn't confident he'll hit everything. He wants to be perfect."

THE PRO COMPETITION EXPLOSION

RIGHT:

IN SOME WAYS, 1993 WORLD PAIR CHAMPIONS FROM CANADA, ISABELLE BRASSEUR AND LLOYD EISLER, CAN CONSIDER THEM- SELVES WINNERS OF THE 1994 OLYMPICS, AS WELL. THOUGH THEY WERE, IN FACT, AWARDED THE BRONZE, THE COU- PLES IN FIRST AND SECOND PLACE WERE RETURNING PROFES- SIONALS, AND, IN THE EYES OF MANY, HAD NO BUSINESS BEING THERE TO BEGIN WITH. BRASSEUR AND EISLER, THEMSELVES, TURNED PRO FOLLOWING THE 1994 SEASON.

OPPOSITE:

ELVIS STOJKO DESPITE WINNING SILVER AT THE SAME GAMES, CHOSE TO STAY ELIGIBLE, AND EXITED THE 1998 OLYMPICS WITH A SECOND SILVER. MANY EXPECTED HIM TO RETIRE AND TURN PROFESSIONAL. YET, IN SPITE OF A GROIN INJURY THAT KEPT HIM AT LESS THAN PEAK CONDI- TION FOR THE SUB- SEQUENT SEASON, AS OF 1999, ELVIS WAS STILL EXPRESS- ING AN INTEREST IN COMPETING AT THE 2002 OLYMPICS.

In 1994, along with their new pros, Candid Productions found themselves encountering competition off, as well as on, the ice. Explains Ribbens, "After 1994, there was this huge boom of competitions, and a lot of other promoters got in the business." The year 1994 saw the addition of numerous professional championships, most of them created to fill a gap in CBS' programming schedule.

The Rock 'n' Roll Championships encouraged its skaters to get down and skate to more eclectic music than was allowed in eligible competition. Appropriately, teenager Oksana Baiul won the ladies' event. Thirty-six-year-old Scott Hamilton won the men's.

The World Team Championship saw Team U.S.A. (Kristi Yamaguchi, Paul Wylie, Urbanski and Marval, and Wynne and Witherby) finishing in second place behind Team Russia (Anna Kondrashova, Alexander Fadeev, Gordeeva and Grinkov, and Usova and Zhulin) and ahead of Team Europe (Katarina Witt, Robin Cousins, Glaser and Rauschenbach, and Torvill and Dean) and Team Canada (Josee Chouinard, Kurt Browning, Brasseur and Eisler, McDonald and Smith). All scores being cumulative, this format favored the best all-around team, rather than a team built around one star. The United States fielded the best woman in the sphere, Kristi Yamaguchi, but their pair team was, at best, third-ranked. Team Europe boasted the best dance team, Torvill and Dean, but a last-place pair team and two singles who, while artistically untouchable, were nowhere near the level of the other ladies and men technically. As a result, Team Russia, with the superior pair, Gordeeva and Grinkov, and

the second best dance team, Usova and Zhulin, was able to overcome the weakness of their singles to win it all.

The Ice Wars in 1994 also featured a team format, with Team U.S.A. (Yamaguchi, Kerrigan, Boitano, and Wylie) easily besting the total strength of the World Team (Witt, Baiul, Browning, and Petrenko).

Unwilling to be left behind during the skating explosion, Dick Button also added a pair of events to his league—the Canadian Pro Championship debuted in December 1994, followed by the U.S. Pro Championship in 1996. A win at the U.S. Pro, Canadian Pro, or Challenge of Champions earned the victor an automatic invitation to the jewel in the crown, the World Pro.

Another 1994 Candid event, the Gold Championship, presented an exclusive field of Olympic gold medalists—and the upset of the decade. Scott Hamilton, with fleet footwork, superb presentation, and not a triple axel in sight, defeated

the man some consider the best jumper ever, Brian Boitano. Before the competition, Scott was quoted as saying, "I can't beat Boitano in the air, so I'll have to beat him on the ground," which he promptly did.

The Gold Championship returned in 1995 and 1996, but in 1997 the event was skipped because of Scott Hamilton's recovery from cancer. Says Ribbens, "We dropped it, because Scott wouldn't have been able to compete, and there is no replacement for Scott."

In 1995, ESPN began broadcasting the Legends Championship, inspired by the classic hypothetical sports question, "If so-and-so had competed against so-and-so, who would have won?" The program's inaugural contest had (in order of finish) Manley, Hamill, Sumners, Zayak, and Tiffany Chin, plus Hamilton, Petrenko, Orser, Wylie, and Beacom. While the "Legend" designation may have been debatable to begin with, (Chin's highest finishes were bronze medals at the 1985 and 1986 Worlds, and Beacom never even won a Canadian title), by 1997 it had lost any luster it might have had, as Lisa-Marie Allen, Scott Williams, and Anita Hartshorn and Frank Sweiding—all skaters without even a national title—were invited to compete.

Another type of event to proliferate in 1995 was the Pro/Am: pros against eligibles. While the format first made an appearance in 1992, with the Pro/Am Challenge, that competition featured only American skaters. The year 1995 saw the initial ISU-initiated international Pro/Am, the Best of the Best, in which

Paul Wylie won $35,000 by defeating eligible Todd Eldredge and finishing second behind Scott Hamilton. Nevertheless, Wylie expressed his displeasure with the entire format, charging that ISU judges, in an attempt to prove that their contest was much tougher than all those nonsanctioned pro competitions, were handing out "tepid" marks of around 5.7 and forcing pro skaters to comply with eligible rules by requiring them to come up with an eight-element short program and limiting their artistic program to under four minutes. Winner Scott Hamilton had problems of his own with the new format, when he learned at the last minute that vocal music would not be allowed. He ended up tossing the program he'd planned to do and revamped a ten-year-old chestnut to fit the requirements. He was also told that his backflip would not be allowed. (But after hearing that he'd won, Hamilton spontaneously did one anyway.)

By 1996, television producers were running low on novel ideas. They'd done team events, head-to-heads, and Pro/Ams. They then tried the Great Skate Debate, with the competition's studio audience playing judge and voting on the winners (Sato won the ladies', Hamilton the men's), and Battle of the Sexes, which matched teams of women (Yamaguchi, Sumners, Manley, and Kadavy) against teams of men (Browning, Hamilton, Wylie, and Boitano). It was hokey. It was a gimmick. It was the highest-rated skating event of the season.

Says ABC's Wilson, "Skating is a marvelous, sweet pie. And when the popularity of it grew to its present level, a heck of a lot more people, driven by a buck, became interested. But the pie didn't get bigger. The quality events didn't get any bigger. So the pie got bigger with created events. Created for not necessarily the good of skating, but for the profit of those who were putting them on. The problem of the burden on the skater to have many more routines is a major consideration."

The increase in the number of competitions presented something of a burden for fans, too. Skating enthusiasts use to spend the entire year looking forward to one or two key events.Now, the most loyal fans found themselves sitting in front of the television practically every evening, watching the same skaters performing the same routines at a glut of nearly identical competitions. As the supply increased, demand for skating seemed to decrease. The fans' boredom with the repetitiveness of the programming showed in a variety of ways, including a decline in television ratings, but it was most visible in the half-empty arenas that now characterize attendance at most professional championships. Only the World Pro continues to sell out regularly.

After a century of drought, after searching for figure skating results in the back of the sports page and scouring *TV Guide* for the odd afternoon special, there were suddenly too many events to keep up with—on television and in person—and not enough fans to attend them all.

As a result, of the sixteen pro competitions taking place in 1996, only nine were still going strong heading into the 1998 Olympics.

Around the Globe on How Many?! Tours

By the 1990s, ice shows had changed from spectacles featuring an anonymous chorus line to more intimate, smaller cast shows filled with familiar Championship faces, such as the Discover Card Stars on Ice ensemble.

Before there was a skating special on television practically every day of the week, fans hoping for a glimpse of their favorite skater outside the Nationals or the World Championship had to wait for a touring show to come to their town.

Ice Capades, Ice Follies, and Holiday on Ice were once the only venues for seeing one or two Olympic-caliber skaters, as long as you were willing to sit through an interminable chorus line and folks dressed as cartoon characters. These were perfect for a family audience, but not nearly as satisfying for the skating purist.

THE COLLINS TOUR

In 1969, a year after television etched Peggy Fleming onto the public's conscious, promoter Tom Collins adjusted Europe's ISU tour of medal winners from the World Championships and brought his new version—featuring both champions and local up-and-comers—to North America. Its first few years out, the Collins Tour (official name pre-1997: Tour of World Figure Skating Champions) visited a scant fifteen cities in the weeks immediately following the World Championships and paid its amateur skaters $50 a show.

By the late 1970s, the tour had solidified its format. Medalists from that year's Worlds, plus a few other skaters judged particularly extraordinary, would perform one number each under spotlights, in front of audiences ranging from five thousand to fifteen thousand people. Little attempt was made to unify the solo exhibitions into a cohesive show format with group numbers. But at the last stop of the 1978 tour, in Providence, Rhode Island, the skaters—including Rodnina and Zaitsev, East Germany's reigning world champion, Anette Potzsch; 1974 world champion Jan Hoffman; Robin Cousins; and Charlie Tickner—put together an impromptu kick-line as an exuberant finale, without telling the show's organizers.

Though only three weeks long, the tour was a great place for young, rising skaters to get a quick lesson in performing in front of a crowd looking to be entertained. Brian Orser, 1984 and 1988 Olympic silver

medalist, admitted to being puzzled his first year on the tour, when he performed the big tricks— triple axel, triple lutz—that drove the public wild in competition and only received polite applause, while Scott Hamilton, dressed in a chicken suit and skating to music peppered with clucks, drove them to a standing ovation.

Brian Boitano joined the tour in 1984, after finishing fifth at the Sarajevo Olympics. By then, skaters were making roughly $150 a show, the maximum these athletes could pocket without risking their amateur status; the compensation would rise with the increase in skating's popularity. For fifteen shows, each skater was paid $2,250, hardly enough to make a dent in the ordinary competitor's expenses. By 1995, however, Olympic-eligible skaters were earning $2,000 per show on a tour that had swelled to seventy-six shows in three months for the spring tour, plus an additional tour in the winter (featuring virtually all pro skaters while the eligibles competed at Nationals, Olympics, and Worlds). A decade after he first joined the redubbed Champions on Ice, the now-pro Boitano earns more than $1 million for his participation.

SKATERS FOLLOW SUIT: NEW TOURS

Established the year Boitano won his first World Championship, Stars on Ice, the brainchild of Scott Hamilton, is a tour restricted to professional skaters that features individual routines as well as group numbers. Originally called Scott Hamilton's America Tour, it played in only five New England towns its first season and starred Hamilton, Toller Cranston, Rosalynn Sumners, and Blumberg and Seibert, along with several lesser-known names. When Discover Card became the principal sponsor a year later, the show became known to fans by that moniker (the same way that Champions on Ice is

still called the Collins Tour and the World Pro is referred to as Landover, after the city where it was presented every year until 1997).

A signature feature of Stars on Ice is its group numbers, where skaters are mixed and matched in combinations the audience might not necessarily expect. Meg Streeter, who directed the show for television from 1992 to 1997, explains, "They take the general premise that you've got a lot of individual great skaters and then [show choreographer] Sandra Bezic does these incredible, innovative group numbers for threesomes or foursomes, whatever feels right at the time, that are also sprinkled throughout the show to give you a sense of family, to create a sense of bonding among the skaters. Kristi [Yamaguchi] and Katarina [Witt] once skated a lovely duet. There was the number where the four women came out, and each one sat on a chair while the other did a solo. What was lovely about that number is Katia [Gordeeva] used to say, 'I love watching Roz [(Sumners) skate.' Four women were out there on the ice, having a good time, and connecting with each other.

WORKING IN A SHOW GAVE SINGLES SKATERS LIKE SCOTT HAMILTON AND BRIAN ORSER A CHANCE TO WORK IN ENSEMBLE NUMBERS.

Those are some of the things that make Stars on Ice special."

Jirina Ribbens praises Hamilton, crediting the ongoing success of Stars on Ice to him. "Scott is unequaled as a performer; he totally understands how to keep the audience in his hand. When he started Stars on Ice, that was his vehicle. He really used turning pro to his advantage. Scott was the first one to have it all."

Along with Stars on Ice, Scott made his stage acting debut in 1989 as the star of Broadway on Ice, where, in addition to skating, he sang his way across the country in a specially written vehicle featuring versions of classic Broadway show routines.

Fellow American Brian Boitano attempted to follow in Scott's footsteps with his tour, Skating, in 1990. With Katarina Witt, Rosalynn Sumners, Underhill and Martini, Caryn Kadavy, Gary Beacom, Blumberg and Seibert, and others, Skating traveled to thirty-one U.S. cities. Like Stars on Ice, it featured group numbers as well as solos ranging from Witt's portrayal of Delilah's seduction and betrayal of Samson to Beacom demonstrating—sans music— his repertoire of funky edges. Skating debuted in Portland to a sold-out audience, a result that was by no means a given, despite the popularity of its stars, since at many venues Skating came to town on the heels of the World Tour. Since Collins' contract with arenas includes a clause forbidding them from advertising another skating show until after the World Tour leaves, fans calling to ask about Skating were often told no information was available.

A year later, Skating II hit the ice with most of the same cast and a "light and dark" theme, wherein the first part of the show featured exclusively light-colored costumes and flowing music and the second half focused on darkness, with black costumes and throbbing, pulsating music. After its third edition,

RIGHT:
ANOTHER ELIGIBLE
SKATER, ELVIS
STOJKO, COULD EVEN
HEADLINE HIS OWN
TOUR WITHOUT
RISKING HIS OLYMPIC
STATUS.

OPPOSITE:
THANKS TO THE
CHANGING OF THE
RULES REGARDING
"AMATEUR" AND
"PROFESSIONAL"
STATUS, AN OLYMPIC-
ELIGIBLE SKATER
LIKE MICHELLE KWAN
COULD PERFORM
ON THE SAME ICE
WITH HER HERO,
PROFESSIONAL
SKATER BRIAN
BOITANO, AND
THE REST OF THE
PROFESSIONAL
CAST OF SKATING
ROMANCE III.

costar for *Skating Romance II*, however, was the always professional Katarina Witt. Arguably the sharpest woman in skating, Katarina is also the one with the highest worldwide profile, based in no small part on the charisma she generates on the ice. With Katarina as his partner, Brian was able to produce a sexier, more adult duet. For *Skating Romance III*, on the other hand, Brian chose to headline with his good pal, teenager Michelle Kwan, leaving choreographers Renee Roca and Gorsha Sur feeling a touch squeamish about putting together one of their traditionally sexy numbers for a seventeen-year-old girl and a man old enough to be her father. But Brian reassured Renee and Gorsha that wasn't what he wanted at all, and so they conceived instead a routine where, in Paris, a giggly Kwan pursues the object of her crush, Boitano, by following him around and aping his every move, including every triple jump. Considering that, in real life, Kwan's first memory of watching skating on television is of Brian winning the 1988 Olympics, the number proved not so far from the truth.

A few years earlier, the notion of an amateur skater like Kwan performing on the same ice as seasoned professionals like Boitano and Roca and Sur would have been inconceivable. By 1997, it was just another one of the perks available to the new eligibles.

During the 1994 Tour of Champions, Canada's Elvis Stojko, world champion in 1994, 1995, and 1997, took even more advantage of the relaxing

the show's producer sold Skating's dates to Stars on Ice, leaving Boitano, after a quick pop back into the eligible world, to branch out into other concepts, including *Skating Romance I, II,* and *III*; *Skating Kicks Back: Country Music and More*; and the *Brian Boitano Holiday Skating Spectacular*, all produced by a production company he could trust—his own, White Canvas. As *Skating Romance*'s artistic director, Brian was also able to insist on a touch cheered by many TV-watching skating purists: he insisted that his show be broadcast with no announcers. He was determined to let the skating stand on its own and speak for itself.

Brian's costar for the inaugural *Skating Romance* was Oksana Baiul, fresh from her triumph in Lillehammer and somewhat unused to life among the pros. Brian was patient, directing and coaxing precisely the performance he desired out of her for their sleepwalking pas de deux to *La Sonambula*. His

rules by coming up with an idea for a tour of his own. Called (what else?) the Elvis Tour, it starred eligible names like Elvis, British champion Steven Cousins, Grishuk and Platov, Bourne and Kraatz, and Kwan, alongside professional stars like Orser, Isabelle Brasseur and Lloyd Eisler, and Liz Manley in a format similar to the one developed by Tom Collins and refined by Stars on Ice. Although he never won Olympic gold, Elvis' popularity in Canada ensured that the stylish tour played to larger and larger audiences each year. In 1997, approximately 100,000 people saw the show in eight cities.

THE ICE SHOWS

For fans of more traditional ice show touring fare, Walt Disney's World on Ice, which purchased Ice Follies and went into business with producer Kenneth Feld, is still the most oriented toward family entertainment. Feld mounted *The Wizard of Oz*, starring 1987 U.S. junior champion Jeri Campbell, and with Disney was the live show producer on *Beauty and the Beast* with Maradith Feinberg and Craig Horowitz, and *Aladdin* with Cynthia Coull, Jamie Eggleton, and 1979 U.S. junior men's champion Jimmy Santee. Adhering to

Hollywood's tradition of replacing Broadway originators with movie-star names when a show went from stage to screen (Audrey Hepburn for Julie Andrews in *My Fair Lady*, Richard Harris for Richard Burton in *Camelot*, Madonna for Patti LuPone in *Evita*), the lead role in *The Wizard of Oz* was skated by Oksana Baiul; in *Beauty and the Beast*, Ekaterina Gordeeva and Viktor Petrenko played the leads; and for *Aladdin*, Kristi Yamaguchi and Kurt Browning were the stars.

Aladdin, a one-hour special for CBS, was taped entirely on location in Cairo, Egypt. Producer Steve Binder was determined to show as much of the countryside as possible, since the last thing he wanted was to go through all the expense of moving company and crew to Africa only to end up with an ice show that looked like it could have been staged on an L.A. lot. That's why his opening montage featured Kristi and Kurt atop a camel riding towards the Pyramids, as well as shots by the Nile and in an outdoor bazaar.

Considering the ancient beauty of the country and the setting of *Aladdin*, it was easy to see why these shots were necessary. It was less easy to figure out why Princess Jasmine and her heroic street urchin were running through all these picturesque locations wearing skates, or why their indoor routines were constantly being interrupted by shots from the movie, breaking the flow of the action and playing up the fact that neither Kristi nor Kurt looked anything like the Disney drawings.

Shooting an ice show is difficult on any location, but in a Muslim country complications arose from the strict edict forbidding the wearing of tight-fitting tops, revealing skirts, or sleeveless shirts for the women, plus the presence of locals, hired as extras, who had never seen sheets of ice before and kept staring at it in wonder. Joked Browning, "They were a good audience, because their expectation of ice was putting it in their drinks."

With the success of the above, Disney's most recent addition to the cartoon-on-ice genre is *Hercules*. They'd already launched *The Spirit of*

Pocahontas, starring Joanna Ng, who in 1991, at the age of twelve, was the youngest-ever winner of Skate Canada. In keeping with the movie's hit song, "Colors of the Wind," eight pair teams plus seven male skaters, each dressed in a distinctive shade, are used to anthropomorphize the invisible element.

Adapting the popular animated film *Toy Story* for the ice brought its own set of challenges. The principal difficulties involved fining ways to bring huge toys to convincing life, including an expanding and contracting Slinky Dog and a skating Mr. Potato Head who can pull his face off at will. The production was unlike the other Disney projects, in other ways as well: *Toy Story* was not a musical, and its solitary female character was Bo Peep. So in

WHILE ICE-VERSIONS
OF THE WIZARD OF
OZ AND TOY STORY
CONTINUE TO EASE
ON DOWN THE ROAD...

contrast with the traditional image of ice shows as starring chorus line after chorus line of gorgeous girls in skimpy outfits, (except for a brief appearance as space sirens), the women of *Toy Story* come out dressed as either soldiers, Martians, or commandos.

In spite—or maybe because—of his success with the Disney productions, not everything Kenneth Feld produces turns to ticket-selling gold. In 1997, he attempted to bring Andrew Lloyd Webber's Broadway musical *Starlight Express*, about roller-skating trains, to the ice. Onstage, the cast sang their own musical numbers and roller-skated straight into the audience. On ice, the skaters lip-synched their warbling and, rather than bringing the show into the audience, brought the audience into the show on four electric flatbed cars parked

right on the edge of the ice. The production was scheduled to tour through the winter of 1998, but poor ticket sales (attributed by some to inadequate publicity, by others to a show that came off as "tacky and childish") prompted it to be pulled around Thanksgiving.

Without a doubt, the biggest skating show loser of 1997 had to be the one historically associated with the ice extravaganza. In 1997, Ice Capades finally folded.

Roughly $40 million in debt, the show first declared bankruptcy in 1993, when it was bought, with momentous fanfare, by former headliner Dorothy Hamill. For more than a year, with herself as the primary star, Hamill attempted to salvage the institution with family-style productions like *Cinderella: Frozen in Time* and *Hansel and Gretel, the Witch, and the Cat*. In 1994, facing personal nd financial problems, she sold Ice Capades to International Family Entertainment, which in turn was purchased, in August 1997, by Rupert Murdoch. He promptly shut down the entire operation.

Ex–Ice Capades manager Dick Palmer told *International Figure Skating* in December 1997 that he blamed the tour's decline on the proliferation of skating shows flooding the marketplace. Ice Capades, which battled to keep ticket prices low so that the whole family might come, just could not keep up. "There was a point that came along when [Olympic and world] champions became so expensive [to hire]. They had their small tours that started getting bigger with Tom Collins and Stars on Ice. The competition became greater when they started doing television specials on ice." Sadly, in the end, the show that first brought skating to everyone's hometown was killed by the popularity it had helped make possible.

THE SHOW MUST GO ON

As escalating ticket prices and the rise in the number of tours made it harder and harder for the average fan to keep up with every ice-company that passed through town, the increase in televised skating specials made it possible for fans to see long-time favorites like 1980 Olympic champion Robin Cousins and 1984 Olympic champion Scott Hamilton more than just once a season.

Television made stars of skaters, and so naturally, television was anxious to capitalize on the new celebrities. Broadcasting competitions and existing tours was an adequate start. But why let someone else call the shots when you can create your own television special and control every aspect of production?

STARS IN THE SPOTLIGHT

Peggy Fleming appeared in her first television spectacular for CBS in 1968, soon after winning the Olympic gold. She would go on to star in many more specials, including one where she got a chance to perform with special guest Gene Kelly.

Dorothy Hamill also kicked up her heels with Kelly in her 1976 post-Olympic *Dorothy Hamill Special*, though the legendary movie star did caution his producers before shooting began in Toronto, "I can't sing like I used to. I certainly can't dance like I used to. And I really can't skate. I'm a triple-threat."

Dorothy and Gene recreated his most famous number, "Singin' in the Rain," with her as the joyful dancer and Gene as the policeman who pops in at the end to spoil her fun. All night, Dorothy skated under a deluge of freezing water, prompting Gene to concede he felt sorry for her. When he filmed the original number, he did it under warm water,

whereas to keep the ice from melting Dorothy's rainstorm had to be bone-chilling. She caught a cold as a result of the shoot; Doug Wilson recalls, "She was really ill, feverish, clammy." She also had an entire symphony orchestra decked out in tuxedos and sitting in a Toronto park where the wind chill was −15°F (−26°C), waiting for Dorothy to come out and skate her second number, "Be a Clown," with Kelly. The producers offered Dorothy the chance to back out but, back straight and shoulders squared, she insisted the show must go on.

Canada's Kurt Browning staged his own tribute to idol Kelly in his special *You Must Remember This*. For his rendition of "Singin' in the Rain," the four-time world champion re-created the set, lighting, costumes, and camera angles of the original so precisely that, on initial viewing, it takes a blink and a moment to realize that the action is taking place on skates.

The first American male skater to get a personal television special, Brian Boitano was already mapping his vision as he moved through the media maze immediately following his 1988 win in Calgary. His fantasy project would involve children and a chance to fulfill his lifelong dream of skating on a glacier. ABC-TV agreed to fund both of those ambitions, but suggested that the definitive Boitano

KATARINA WITT HAS TAKEN CONTROL OF HER CAREER LIKE FEW FEMALE ATHLETES BEFORE HER—AND CHANGED THE BUSINESS OF SKATING IN THE PROCESS. HERE SHE APEARS WITH CO-STAR CHRISTOPHER BARKER IN THE FEATURE FILM ICE PRINCESS.

special include an appearance by Katarina Witt. The 1984 and 1988 Olympic champion from East Germany was eager to participate. Her political influence was at its zenith, and after months of negotiations, Katarina received government permission to take part in the American project. But while her government was telling Katarina that permission had been granted, they were telling ABC that permission had been denied. Finally, on Labor Day, 1988, a conference call was set up between ABC, Brian Boitano, and Katarina Witt—phoning from the commissar's office—so that the politically savvy Witt could monitor what was being said by and to all the participating parties.

Once the battle to shoot in East Germany was won, the ABC staff wondered just what they'd gotten themselves into with this unprecedented project. The rink itself presented a challenge.

Remembers Wilson, "We had minimum facilities, we were in a drab, East German, not-sensually moti-vating rink, and we had to do very dramatic, very theatrical things on a venue that had no quality related to that."

Wilson and choreographer Sandra Bezic, of whom Wilson says, "She's the most beautiful genius I've ever met, and you can quote me," racked their brains trying to figure out how they were going to transform a cold, unsightly rink into the site of Brian and Katarina's hot-blooded ice tryst. Finally, a decision was made to flood the set with as much light as possible, blurring the background until they created a practically animated, stop-action, smoky effect. Wilson admits, "You wouldn't want to watch skating like that all the time, but in the context of the piece, it isn't bad. The emotions that came out of it were genuine."

MOVIE STAR GENE KELLY WAS AN INSPIRATION TO NUMEROUS SKATERS. PEGGY FLEMING, DOROTHY HAMILL, AND KURT BROWNING ALL GOT TO SKATE THEIR TRIBUTES TO HIM, AND 1980 OLYMPIC CHAMPION ROBIN COUSINS ONCE REMARKED, "GROWING UP, I DIDN'T WANT TO BE AN ATHLETE. I WANTED TO BE GENE KELLY."

The success of the Boitano/Witt pairing prompted their reunion to film *Carmen on Ice*. Released as a theatrical feature in Europe and shown in the U.S. on HBO, *Carmen on Ice* broke new ground for televised ice ballets, in that portions of the movie were shot on location in Seville, Spain, including in a bullfighting ring. (Portable ice rinks were buried at ground level, then painted over to blend in with the surroundings.) Along with costar Brian Orser, Boitano and Witt won Emmy Awards for Outstanding Individual Performance. Joked Boitano, "Here I spend twenty years working for an Olympic gold medal and my first year out I win an Emmy!"

Figuring that if one Olympic champion was good and two even better, then an entire contingent would have to be ratings gold, ABC presented *Skates of Gold* in 1993, billing it as a one-time gathering of past Olympic winners in each of the four disciplines. Three dance teams performed, along with four ladies, three pairs, and four men. Among the nonskating highlights was a chance to see Irina Rodnina wave to the crowd alongside both of her former partners, Alexei Ulanov and Alexander Zaitsev.

In 1994, NBC broadcast *Skates of Gold II*, with medalists from the Lillehammer Games as part of the cast. In 1995, the one-time event returned to ABC for *Skates of Gold III*, although by then the fellowship was visibly shrinking. In the pairs, Valova and Vasiliev's divorce and Mishkutenok and Dmitriev's breakup left only Gordeeva and Grinkov to represent the discipline. In dance, Torvill and Dean's exclusive agreement with CBS allowed them to skate in the show, but prevented ABC from showing their performance or the team from skating out to take their bows alongside the rest of the cast, leaving viewers in the arena and at home to wonder what the British champions had done to warrant such banishment.

Another once-in-a-lifetime event that somehow stretched into a three-parter was *Symphony of Sports*. In 1989, the Women's Sports Foundation conceived a fund-raiser where skating and gymnastics would share the stage. For one night only, Brian Boitano, Robin Cousins, Underhill and Martini, and Rosalynn Sumners were joined by Olympic gymnasts Bart Conner, Marcia Frederick, Kristi Phillips, and Peter Vidmar. A mat was laid on the ice, leaving the skaters to maneuver around it in a V-configuration without tripping into the audience and the gymnasts to tumble on a smaller-than-average square without slipping off onto the frozen water.

AFTER TAPING THEIR STEAMY <u>CARMEN</u> BALLET FOR CABLE TV, BRIAN BOITANO AND KATARINA WITT TOURED THE COUNTRY WITH EXCERPTS FROM THE SHOW. THE CHEMISTRY BETWEEN THEM PROMPTED NUMEROUS FANS TO FANTASIZE A ROMANTIC RELATIONSHIP BETWEEN THE PAIR.

THE CANADIAN
CURSE: ALTHOUGH
CANADIAN CHAMPI-
ONS HAVE ALWAYS
BEEN A FORCE TO BE
RECKONED WITH ON
THE INTERNATIONAL
SCENE, THEY HAVE
SEEN LITTLE
OLYMPIC GLORY. LIKE
BRIAN ORSER AND
ELVIS STOJKO, 1983
WORLD CHAMPION
ROSALYNN SUMNERS
WAS UNABLE TO
BRING HOME THE
GOLD, SETTLING FOR
THE SILVER MEDAL IN
1984.

For many, the highlight of the program came in a romantic duet between Cousins on the ice and, on the mat, Katherine Healy, a twenty-year-old ballerina best known for acting in the movie *Six Weeks* (with Mary Tyler Moore and Dudley Moore) and being featured in the children's book *A Very Young Skater*. Because she'd been a skater as well as a dancer, when Cousins briefly lifted her off the mat for a swoop around the ice, Healy knew how to hold her position, thereby creating a seamless transition and a perfect blending of the two art forms, something the other gymnasts, with all their varied skills, simply could not do. Wilson adds another reason why that number is the one viewers remember best: "Robin is very much a producer as well as a skater. And so to work with him was a pleasure because he created [that pas de deux] especially for the camera."

Another treat for skating fans came at the conclusion of the *Symphony of Sports* when 1984 Olympian Bart Conner put on a pair of skates and performed a mean set of butterflies, holding hands with Roz Sumners. A year later, Bart's soon-to-be wife, Nadia Comaneci, joined the company of a –second *Symphony of Sports*, and the year after that, Peggy Fleming, Brian Orser, and Peter and Kitty Carruthers contributed their talents to a third show. In the latter, Orser got to take center stage as a leather-jacketed 1950s rocker inspiring starry-eyed swoons from a gaggle of giggling gymnasts and skaters, including Fleming, dressed as a bobby-soxer waitress, who literally backflips for Orser (with a little help from a muscular gymnast) in a move that, during rehearsal, required much nervous shrieking before actually being executed for the first time.

While events like *Skates of Gold* and *Symphony of Sports* were, without a doubt, gimmicky, they at least offered original ideas as rationale for putting on yet another skating show. By the mid-1990s, with everyone eager to put an icy display on the air, even inventive ideas had shrunk to a minimum, leaving made-for-TV offerings like *Too Hot to Skate*, where a Santa Cruz, California, boardwalk parking lot was turned into an ice surface, and thirty-five hundred spectators packed the hastily erected stands to watch an offering—the premise of which seemed to be "It's summer, but people are skating. Isn't that interesting?"

It wasn't. But that didn't stop producers from following up with *Too Hot To Skate II*.

TRIBUTES, CELEBRATIONS, AND REQUIEMS

Eventually, even misery, illness, and death proved to be plausible premises for yet another skating special. The first came in 1996, when CBS aired *A Celebration of a Life*, in honor of Sergei Grinkov, dead at the age of twenty-eight from a heart attack suffered while practicing with his partner and wife, Ekaterina Gordeeva.

Following ABC's determination to baptize her the media sprite of the 1988 Olympics, "Katia" reigned as skating's darling, while Sergei was...the guy next to her. Television cameras shooting the pair somehow managed always to zoom in on Katia's smile, Katia in a lift, Katia in a spin. Even live, there was no reason to watch Sergei. He was the exemplary partner—strong, silent, unobtrusive. He could be counted on to be there when Katia needed him to throw her or catch her or present her to the audience. He never made a mistake (except during the long program at the 1994 Olympics, where he

popped a double salchow into a single. That performance was his least favorite and, ironically, the one that television kept airing over and over after his death). For years, everpresent cameras caught little Katia tailing behind Sergei, a look of complete adoration on her face, while he appeared barely aware of her existence. Then, away from the cameras' prying eyes, Katia and Sergei fell in love, married, and became parents of a daughter, Daria.

On November 20, 1995, the love story crashed to an end.

Immediately, the skating world wondered: what would Katia do? She'd lost not only her husband and the father of her child but, it seemed, her professional future as well. Half of a pair team might as well be half of nothing. The cast of Stars on Ice, which Gordeeva and Grinkov had been touring with, gathered to offer Katia their support, as did her friends in Simsbury, Connecticut, where she and Sergei had made their home. Everyone was eager to shelter and protect the fragile new widow. It was exactly then that the five-foot-one-inch (155cm), ninety-pound (41kg) sprite proceeded to show the world precisely what she was made of.

In the past, there'd been glimpses of Katia's hidden strength. As evidenced in their practices at the 1985 World Junior Championship (which they won), it was obvious that tiny Katia ran the team. At the 1988 World Championships, television analyst Scott Hamilton remarked, "She is really the foundation of this pair. I watched a practice session recently, and I watched her put her partner and her coach through a training session that would put a Washington Redskin on his knees." When they turned professional and began spending more of their time in the States, Katia, whose English was better than her husband's, became the spokesperson for both. A smart and savvy young woman, she quickly figured out exactly what the media needed to hear from her, and made certain to give them just what they wanted, not only translating a reporter's questions from English to Russian for Sergei but,

WHEN SHE TURNED TO SINGLES SKATING AFTER THE DEATH OF HER HUSBAND AND PARTNER, EKATERINA GORDEEVA ADMITTED THAT SHE DIDN'T HAVE THE JUMPING SKILLS OF OTHER WOMEN. BUT, FANS IN LOVE WITH THE "KATIA" LEGEND WERE SO ENAMORED OF HER MAGICAL ON-ICE PRESENCE AND CHARMING PERSONALITY, THE NUMBER OF REVOLUTIONS IN HER JUMPS DIDN'T REALLY MATTER.

when interpreting his answers from Russian to English, editing them to better fit their image. As a result of Katia's flawless PR skills and fabulous smile, she and Sergei soon became the most popular Russian skaters in the U.S.

The genuine esteem they inspired among fans, as well as their Stars on Ice colleagues, was evident at the February 1996 performance of *A Celebration of a Life*, the skating show that would be edited into a television special. Along with the Stars on Ice cast, skating in honor of Sergei's memory were Oksana Baiul, Brian Boitano, Yuka Sato, Klimova and Ponomarenko, Viktor Petrenko, Alexandr Fadeev, and Fedor Andreev, the thirteen-year-old son of

Katia and Sergei's choreographer, Marina Zoueva. Fedor was born the year Gordeeva and Grinkov started skating together, and he fondly recalled Sergei telling him not to whine before a practice session "because the practice just isn't going to get any shorter."

Zoueva also choreographed the solo number Katia skated the night of the tribute. Set to Mahler's "Adagietto," it was a heartwrenching reenactment of love, loss, and rebirth, made even more haunting by the fact that the program wasn't really a solo number, but rather a pair routine for one. In numerous places, it was noticeable Katia wasn't alone on the ice, as her body positions suggested a phantom presence holding and urging her on. Afterward, Katia confirmed the impression, telling the crowd, "I want you to know that I skated today not alone. I skated with Sergei. It's why it was so good. And it wasn't me."

Sergei's presence was also felt, equally implicitly, in the 1997 television special *Snowden on Ice*. In this hour-long CBS fairy tale, Katia portrayed a single mother, Kate, who, with her young daughter, Lizzie (Daria Grinkova), moves back to her hometown, the site of a humiliating childhood skating competition that made Kate swear off ice forever. Scott Hamilton (who coproduced) narrates the story in his role as an all-knowing Zamboni driver, and Kurt Browning plays the local hockey coach, who first teases, then falls in love with the local figure skating coach, Josee Chouinard. (In a typical chauvinistic attitude, all the kids in the hockey club are boys and all the children in the figure skating club are girls. While the boys laugh and play and goof around to upbeat, cheerful music, the girls jump and spin to a droning metronome and lyrics nagging how they must practice constantly, with no time for anything else.) In the week prior to *Snowden's* airing, the show received rather mediocre reviews, with many critics wondering about the ethics of capitalizing on Katia's sad story for entertainment (and a very active tie-in campaign with Target stores), as well as the seeming exploitation of Daria—besides appearing in the movie, she also posed for a milk ad, and numerous magazine covers with her mother, as well as an unending stream of television up-close-and-personal pieces, prompting one producer to dub her "the ultimate prop."

Despite the criticism, CBS continued to mine the Gordeeva and Grinkov story. Based on Katia's *New York Times* best-selling book, *My Sergei*, the docudrama featured competition (including early World Junior Championships), show and news footage, interviews with Stars on Ice costars, home movies, family pictures, and reenactments of such never-filmed events as Katia and Sergei's first tryout as a pair, Sergei skating with an injured Katia in his

arms, and their first kiss in a sauna. The skater Katia personally picked to portray Sergei in the reenactments was Anton Sikharulidze, who both skates and looks like Sergei—so much so that at the 1998 Nagano Olympics, observers remarked that it was eerie to see Katia and Anton sitting side by side in the stands to watch the competition, chatting and laughing.

Katia's involvement with *My Sergei* led to a genuinely tasteful production, unlike the two low-budget, exploitative made-for-television movies that chronicled the life of Oksana Baiul and the story of Nancy Kerrigan and Tonya Harding. In *A Promise Kept: The Oksana Baiul Story*, an arena in Pittsburgh served as every ice rink in the world, while footage was cut indiscriminately and with little apparent concern for continuity, from Monica Keena, the actress portraying Oksana, to Baiul doing her own skating. In *Tonya and Nancy: The Real Story*, actors playing actual personalities from the sensational Kardigan episode spoke directly into the camera, explaining the tale in the most simplistic terms possible rather than fully dramatizing it.

ALTHOUGH DARIA GRINKOVA, DAUGHTER OF EKATERINA GORDEEVA AND SERGEI GRINKOV, HAS TAKEN SOME SKATING LESSONS, HER MOTHER ADMITS IT WAS SERGEI'S DREAM THAT HIS LITTLE GIRL STUDY...KARATE!

In 1997, Rudy Galindo sold his autobiography, *Icebreaker*, to Showtime for production as a movie, adding that he thought Johnny Depp playing him would be "really cool". Hopefully, if and when *Icebreaker* makes it to the small screen, it will follow in the mold not of Tonya and Nancy or Oksana Baiul, but of *My Sergei*, a moving and beautiful retrospective of a life.

Another memorial, *A Skaters' Tribute to Carlo Fassi*, aired on ESPN in 1997 in honor of the legendary coach who died at the World Championship that March. The man who guided Peggy Fleming, Dorothy Hamill, John Curry, and Robin Cousins to Olympic gold, Jill Trenary to a World Championship, and Caryn Kadavy to a world bronze was at the 1997 Worlds with his U.S. bronze medalist, Nicole Bobek, when he suffered a heart attack.

A two-time European champion, the Italian Fassi, with his wife, Christa, came to America in 1961, following the plane crash that wiped out not only the United States' champions but many of its top coaches as well. His first notable student was Peggy Fleming, a girl whom Carlo once described as his most talented pupil (and his laziest). According to Carlo, by the time Peggy finished fixing her hair, stretching her legs, and skating a few warmup laps, the forty-five-minute practice session would be almost over. But when competition time came and she knew she had to deliver, she did. Fleming came with another component: her mother, whom some likened to Mama Rose from *Gypsy*, while others saw her as her daughter's greatest advocate. Every night during the years Peggy trained with Carlo, Mrs. Fleming would call the Fassi home, often during dinnertime, and engage Carlo in an hourlong— sometimes longer—discussion of her daughter's progress that day and of his plans for their session tomorrow. Realizing this could take a while, Christa would prop a pillow under Carlo's head and give him a blanket so that he could stretch out along their kitchen counter and rest while Mrs. Fleming spoke. At his memorial service in Switzerland, a

tearful Peggy predicted that the moment Carlo got to heaven, there would be a ring of the phone, and her mother would be on the other end.

It was while instructing Peggy that Carlo pioneered the team teaching technique used at many training sites today. Besides his wife, without whom Carlo swears he never could have achieved the results he did, he invited various choreographers to contribute to Peggy's programs. Said Carlo, "You must have a team, because not everyone can be good at everything. One coach may be technically good and not have the personality to bring out a champion."

If there was one thing Carlo Fassi had in spades, it was personality. At any competition, he was the best show in town. A gregarious man who knew everyone from every association, he could most often be found in the hotel lobby, smoking and holding court. He sat back and let the acolytes come to him. Skaters, judges, federation heads, television staffers—they all wanted to hear what Carlo

THIRTY-TWO YEARS AFTER SHE WON HER FIRST WORLD CHAMPIONSHIP, PEGGY FLEMING WAS STILL GOING STRONG, PERFORMING IN ESPN'S BROADCAST OF SKATER'S TRIBUTE TO HOLLYWOOD.

thought of the upcoming competition, who Carlo thought would win, who Carlo thought they should keep an eye on. Carlo answered every question graciously, offering a joke here, an anecdote there, and then he was off to the rink to oversee his students' practice, to help them in any way he could—be it through body language or shouted instructions in broken English or pounding the barrier with skateguards to boost their energy—to squeeze out one more jump or one more spin than their exhausted bodies ever dreamed possible.

In 1976, Carlo coached both the men's Olympic gold medalist, John Curry, and the women's, Dorothy Hamill. Neither win was the shoo-in Peggy had been eight years earlier. John had only been third at the World Championship the year before, and Dorothy second. Neither came in as the favorite, and both were well known for their nerve-induced inconsistency. About Dorothy, Carlo said, "She was always second or third at Worlds, but it was a good thing. She didn't have the pressure of trying to hold the title."

Many of the skaters who turned to Carlo went looking for help with their compulsory figures, so it was enormously appropriate that his final world champion, the United States' Jill Trenary, would also be the last ladies' champion to be crowned because of a combined score of figures and free-skating. (In fact, Trenary, who finished fifth in the short program and second in the long program, beat out Japan's Midori Ito, who won both the short and the long, only because Jill won the figures.) With the television-prompted demise of the figures, Carlo's conveyer belt of champions slowed to a crawl.

Carlo moved back to his native Italy for several years, then returned to the States in 1994 to coach at the Ice Castle International Training Center. There, Carlo was reunited with a pupil he had first spotted in 1983, when the mischievous six-year-old, despite seeing that the great Carlo Fassi was in the middle of giving a lesson, brazenly hit the ice and proceeded to skate circles around him, showing off axel after axel until he had to pay attention to her.

VETERAN COACH CARLO FASSI'S LAST HOME WAS THE ICE CASTLE INTERNATIONAL TRAINING CENTER, WHERE TWO-TIME OLYMPIC BRONZE MEDALIST LU CHEN ONCE TRAINED.

THE SHOW MUST GO ON

117

At the end of the session, Carlo asked the tiny whirlwind her name.

"Nicole Bobek," she proudly told him.

By age ten, Nicole was training with Carlo full-time. She even followed him to Italy for a few months, but the circumstances of living in Europe didn't work out. When they reunited in 1996, Nicole was at the lowest point ever in her skating career. She'd gone through a succession of coaches, lost her national title, and failed to qualify for the 1996 World Team. It was Carlo who, with a combination of pedagogical firmness and paternal concern, whipped her back into shape, coaching Nicole to a bronze medal at the 1997 U.S. Championships. When he died at the World Championships, a big part of Nicole's confidence died with him, as, after a night of no sleep, Nicole stumbled to an error-filled thirteenth-place finish.

Yet as another former Fassi pupil, Robin Cousins, observed at the tribute show staged in Carlo's honor at the California Training Center, where he'd spent his last years, by August everyone who'd loved the man was finished grieving and was ready to celebrate his life with a smile.

And there were certainly plenty of smiles in the three days of preparation before the show, as thirty years of Fassi apprentices gathered to reminisce and throw a party in his memory. Paul Wylie, the 1992 Olympic silver medalist, whom Fassi coached to the 1981 World Junior Championship, recalled how Carlo, in an attempt to calm down his protégés prior to competition, would thrust his face inches from theirs and shout, "Relax!" The five-foot-four-inch (163cm) Wylie also related that it

was Fassi who, deciding on a whim in the late 1970s that Paul should skate pairs, introduced him to Dana Graham, and ordered them to start practicing lifts right away. He balanced Dana on the barrier and told Paul to hold her up. The teenage Paul tried his best, but as soon as Carlo let go, so did Paul. In spite of that less than auspicious beginning, Graham and Wylie went on to win the 1980 U.S. Junior Pair Championship before calling it quits.

At the tribute, Paul skated "Bring Him Home" from the musical *Les Misérables*; Peggy Fleming presented "Ave Maria"; Nicole Bobek performed "Sacrifice" and a rather interesting choice for a memorial, "You Don't Own Me"; and Robin Cousins rewrote the lyrics to Gershwin's "They Can't Take That Away from Me." Yet for many, the most moving moment of the night came at the finale, when all

A month later, the skating show, along with a *Biography*-style profile of the man, aired on ESPN as the two-hour *Skaters' Tribute to Carlo Fassi*. Yet one story missing from both the live and the television show was of a seventeen-year-old junior skater who, in 1976, was ready to give up the sport because his family simply could not afford it any longer. When Fassi, who was interested in coaching the boy himself, heard about his dilemma, he lined up a sponsor to take care of his training and expenses. The news so cheered the teen up that he went on to win the 1976 U.S. Junior Championship.

of Carlo's Olympic champions (save Curry, who had died in 1994), his world champions (except Trenary, who was recovering from surgery but had flown in to be in the audience), his national medalists, including Wylie, Caryn Kadavy, Angelo D'Agostino, Tom Dickson (who was representing himself and wife, Catarina Lindgren, home awaiting the birth of their twins), John Baldwin, Jr. (representing himself and his father, both national novice champions under Carlo), and various others, took the ice at the same time. From 1968 Olympic champ Peggy Fleming to 1998 Olympic hopeful Nicole Bobek, they all turned as one to salute Carlo's portrait beaming down at them from above the ice.

It was a gathering that couldn't have happened a few years earlier, when amateurs and professionals were forbidden to share the same ice. Now, the current rule changes had made possible this tearfully appropriate, once-in-a-lifetime tribute.

Scott Hamilton was on his way to the top.

Three years later, Scott left the Fassis and headed east. To Carlo, he would always be the one that got away. In spite of their parting, there was speculation prior to the tribute that Scott might come to at least watch, but sadly, in the summer of 1997, Scott Hamilton had problems of his own.

He was diagnosed with testicular cancer a few days before Fassi's death in March, leaving the dazed skating community at the 1997 World Championships walking around shell-shocked, wondering what tragedy would strike next. At the time of Fassi's tribute, Hamilton was off the ice, recovering from surgery and chemotherapy. Skating's high profile ensured that the story got mountains of media coverage, including a cover story in *People* and—the ultimate sign that your sport has entered superstar stratospheres—a mention in the *National Enquirer*. (Previously, the mainstream press' interest in ailing skaters was limited to

JUST AS THE RULES OF PROFESSIONAL SKATING CHANGED YET AGAIN, PAUL WYLIE TOOK HIS LEAVE FROM THE COMPETITION. PLANS FOR 1999 INCLUDED HARVARD BUSINESS SCHOOL AND MARRIAGE TO GIRLFRIEND KATE PRESBY.

THESE PAGES:
AS THEY HAD A FEW
YEARS EARLIER FOR
SERGEI GRINKOV'S
TRIBUTE, THE CAST
OF STARS ON ICE
GOT TOGETHER TO
CELEBRATE A MUCH
HAPPIER OCCASION—
SCOTT HAMILTON'S
RETURN TO THE
ICE AFTER BEATING
CANCER.

the morbidly gleeful death-from-AIDS body count kept by several major newspaper reporters.) Scott's illness, or rather his recovery, proved a good enough reason to stage yet another skating telecast, and on October 29, 1997, CBS taped *Scott Hamilton: Back on the Ice*. With celebrity guests Jack Nicholson, Cindy Crawford, Leeza Gibbons, and Angie Dickinson to add Hollywood glamour to the occasion, and proceeds going to the Cleveland Clinic Foundation, which treated Hamilton's cancer, the star-studded

night climaxed with Scott's tear-jerking performance to Gary Morris' live rendition of "With One More Look at You."

Unbeknownst to Scott's fans, who only saw the show live or broadcast, Scott's true comeback occurred during the rehearsal for that final number. It happened with no fanfare or warning. At the main rehearsal, just as the television people were settling down and getting ready to begin, Gary Morris ascended the artists' platform and proceeded to perform his song so that audio could get a level check. No cameras were rolling. With no warning, Scott stepped out onto the ice and began skating his number. It wasn't officially a run-through. Everyone was supposed to be doing something else. No one was supposed to be watching the ice, yet everybody in the arena knew something magical was taking place. Everybody in the arena stopped what they were doing and watched, mesmerized, comprehending that this, truly, was the moment of Scott's return.

One of the most interesting portions of the televised show came when some of the world's best skaters each attempted to re-create a part of one of Scott's most popular routines, pointing out, once and for all, what made the 1984 Olympic gold medalist so irreplaceable.

After the entire cast rocked out to "Hair," Paul Wylie kicked things off with his homage to Scott's "Conductor" routine. However, Wylie's precise, fastidious style seemed out of place in a program whose primary theme is a skater growing more and more tired until he finally loses so much control he can barely stand after a spin. Next, Rosalynn Sumners came out in Scott's blue-with-red-V Olympic costume, skating to "You Always Hurt the One You Love," followed by Kristi Yamaguchi

hopscotching through "When I'm 64." Despite her technical skills (she did an axel with a hat pinned to her vest), Kristi came off more as an authentic little girl rather than the adult briefly hiding in the childhood of Scott's interpretation. Brian Orser delivered "Cuban Pete" with the backflip in the right place but without anything like the right facial expression, while Brian Boitano couldn't stop grinning all through his "In the Mood" while dressed in a chicken suit. Neither Orser nor Boitano managed to recapture Scott's sheer joy in his own silliness, so necessary for both programs. Similarly, Ekaterina Gordeeva, performing Scott's spoof of the lounge lizard who sings "I Love Me," was handicapped by the shortage of Las Vegas entertainers in Russia. n the end, Kurt Browning's "Walk This Way" came the closest to not just imitating Scott's steps but capturing his exuberant spirit, suggesting that when, a long, long, long time from now, Hamilton is ready to retire his spot as the greatest entertainer that skating ever saw, Canada's four-time world champion might prove the most logical replacement.

In the end one thing is certain: when the changing of the guard finally does occur, television will inevitably be on hand, ready to package it into a prime-time special for everyone to see.

The Russians Arrive

In the early 1990s, Russian-born Gorsha Sur (pictured with partner Renee Roca, opposite) trained in the United States, to represent the United States. His example was, apparently, contagious. By the time the 1999 Russian Nationals rolled around, half the skaters on the podium were training in America. Yet, in 1998, for reasons of loyalty, 1994 Olympic champion Alexei Urmanov (above) chose to launch his comeback, after an injury-plagued year, from the same St. Petersburg rink he'd always trained at.

During the days when Americans were still called "amateurs," the only professionals entered in the Olympics were from the Soviet republic. Even though most put down generalities like "student" or "soldier" under "occupation," the majority never saw the inside of either a university classroom or an artillery range. Instead, fully supported by the State, they practiced full-time to achieve the single goal for which they were to do the one thing they were trained—to skate and earn glory for their country.

AN EMPIRE CRUMBLES

However, the end of the Soviet Union also meant an end to the special privileges—the apartments, nutritious food, unlimited ice time, lessons, and costumes—accorded elite athletes. It meant an end to the support.

Almost immediately, the legendary training centers began to collapse into disarray. At the once-mighty Yubilany Rink in St. Petersburg, Olympic

RADKA KOVARIKOVA AND HUSBAND RENE NOVATNY WERE CZECHOSLOVAKIA'S FIRST PAIR WORLD CHAMPIONS—AND ITS LAST. SINCE THEIR WIN IN 1995, THE COUNTRY HAS CEASED TO EXIST.

champion Alexei Urmanov describes the ice as "sometimes too hard, sometimes too soft, sometimes just water." At the rink in Odessa in the Ukraine, when a cooling pipe burst, the management, instead of fixing it, just put up a barrier and ordered the skaters training there, including 1996 European champion Viacheslav Zagorodnik, to "skate around it." In 1994, Olympic champion Viktor Petrenko donated $15,000 to upgrade his old training base. It took three years for the money to show up (according to Zagorodnik, it went into "someone's pocket") and for a few of the critical repairs to get done. Interest in skating is at such a low in the former Soviet Republic that Zagorodnik has taken to handing out his publicity photos wherever he goes. "When I go to the store, when police pull me over for speeding, I just hand them a flyer." In 1998, Zagorodnik gave up and relocated to West Virginia. Said Zagorodnik, "America is where the skating work is."

In 1997, Tamara Moskvina, coach of Bereznaia and Sikharulidze, and Kazakova and Dmitriev, was desperately looking for a new training site when Yubilany announced it would be closing for renovations so that the rink could host the year 2000 Hockey World Championship. Deprived of ice, she and her teams spent the summer of 1998 training in the United States.

Rivals in the West couldn't help feeling some sense of satisfaction at the sudden change of fortune. Now, finally, Eastern skaters would learn what it's like to battle hockey players for ice, to work two jobs to pay for lessons, to stretch old boots an extra half-size and make them last another season. In 1992, Alexei Mishin complained, "I need skates for my boy [Alexei Urmanov]. The boots he has now are ready to fall apart. We need money from the Russian federation. Money they don't have." Marina Khalturina, a pairs skater who once trained in Moscow but now represents Kazakhstan, echoes the complaint: "We sent a bill for our skates to the federation. But we're not holding our breath waiting for reimbursement."

Despite the terrible training conditions back in Russia, it quickly began to seem as if their Western rivals had smirked too soon. Just as reports of Mark Twain's death were greatly exaggerated, so too were reports of the death of the Soviet pre-eminence in skating. In spite of their shortage of money and ice, Russians still managed to win every discipline at the 1997 and 1998 European Championships. At the 1998 Olympics, they won the gold and silver in ice dance, the gold and silver in pairs, and the gold in men's.

These impressive statistics are so dazzling that they easily obscure a startling realization: that the role of the former Union of Soviet Socialist Republics as primary sponsor for figure skaters from the former Soviet republics has now in many cases been taken over by the American taxpayer.

AID TO FORMER SOVIETS

The fall fo the Soviet Union created a number of confusing situations in the skating world, not least, the exchange of U.S. funds for former Soviet training. The new era began in 1992, when the Lake Placid Olympic Training Center—under sponsorship of the New York State Olympic Regional Development Authority (ORDA) and Governor George Pataki—invited Natalia Dubova, coach of the 1992 Olympic bronze medalists Usova and Zhulin, to head their new Lake Placid International Ice Dancing School. The idea was that by having Russian coaches training U.S. athletes, Americans would finally get a peek at the techniques that earned the Soviets forty-one world medals in ice dancing and would thereby become better ice dancers. Of course, in order to attract a coach of

ALEXANDER ZHULIN'S EARLY '90S AFFAIR WITH OKSANA GRISHUK SO UPSET HIS WIFE AND PARTNER, MAIA USOVA (PICTURED, ABOVE, WITH ZHULIN), THAT IT PROMPTED THEIR COACH, NATALIA DUBOVA (BELOW), TO SEND GRISHUK BACK TO MOSCOW, AND PAIR GRISHUK'S PARTNER, EVGENY PLATOV, WITH TATIANA NAVKA. YET, BY THE END OF THE DECADE, AND MANY TITLES AND COACHES AND COUNTRIES LATER, PLATOV WAS SKATING WITH USOVA, AND ZHULIN WAS SKATING WITH GRISHUK—WHILE DATING TATIANA NAVKA.

Dubova's stature to Lake Placid, the facility offered lavish compensation. In addition to her salary, Dubova is guaranteed that up to four of her foreign couples may skate at the training center free of charge. Housing is also part of the package for Dubova's protégés. When they first arrived in the United States, Kazakhstani dancers Stekolnikova and Kazarliga were put up by ORDA in the training center's dormitories. Dubova's top couple, Usova and Zhulin, were also offered housing.

Through ORDA, the Lake Placid Olympic Training Center receives the bulk of its funding from the U.S. Olympic Committee, as well as from the town of North Elba, New York, whose residents donate $60,000 annually. These funds come from local taxpayers and from private citizens contributing to the U.S. Olympic Committee.

Meanwhile, at the University of Delaware in Newark, Natalia Linichuk and Gennadi Karpanosov coach their Russian teams on "international ice" forbidden to American couples. In exchange for agreeing to skate in a few shows a year to benefit the university's skating program, Russian skaters receive six hours of ice time a day plus housing. Again, the thinking is that having Russian coaches on-site will cultivate America's dance program. So far, however, like Dubova in New York, Linichuk has yet to produce a single American dance team that's medaled nationally, much less internationally,

above the novice level.

American pair skaters Urbanski and Marval, "the Waitress and the Truck Driver," complained to *Blades on Ice* in September 1995 about the situation in Delaware, their former training site: "You have [Russian] teams that were given free houses. Our tax dollars are paying for it."

Similar situations exist at training centers across the United States. In Marlboro, Massachusetts, Tatiana Tarasova coached Russian, Ukrainian, and Italian dancers, and Russian and French freestyle skaters like Ilia Kulik, Alexei Yagudin, and Surya Bonaly through the summer of 1998, then relocated to New Jersey. Irina Rodnina coached her 1995 world pair champions from the Czech Republic, Kovarikova and Novatny, while she was at Lake Arrowhead, California. Lake Arrowhead is also the home base of Klimova and Ponomarenko, the ice dancers who, in 1994, agreed to instruct Canadian champions Bourne and Kraatz along with local American teams, but were soon too busy with their other professional commitments, tours, and shows, in the view of some, to fulfill their agreement satisfactorily. In Simsbury, Connecticut, Galina Zmievskaya's presence guarantees free ice for her students, including Olympic champions Viktor Petrenko and Ekaterina Gordeeva.

These conditions have prompted accusations of unfairness from many parts of the skating world.

American skaters, for example, resent their competitors being given for free what some U.S. athletes have sold their houses for, while American coaches resent foreigners being subsidized by other Americans to come in and take their students.

The Soviet Union paid all the expenses necessary for skaters like Klimova and Ponomarenko, Viktor Petrenko, and Oksana Baiul to get to the top. No sooner had these skaters pocketed their gold medals, than the rules changed; with the Soviet Union no longer in power, the skaters were free to earn money for skating professionally. They promptly took advantage of this by moving to the United States and choosing from among the offers of Americans eager to pay them just to skate at their facilities.

RUSSIANS FOR HIRE

Another consequence of the Soviet Union's collapse—prompting further complaints of unfairness in American skating circles—is a practice colloquially dubbed "Rent-a-Russian."

In 1993, when Russian-born Gorsha Sur won the first of two U.S. dance titles with his American partner, Renee Roca, he planted an idea in the heads of dozens of girls desperately looking for a boy to skate with: the boy they were looking for didn't necessarily have to be American. Unfortunately, a distinction was lost along the way. Sur settled in the U.S. legitimately, as a defector looking for freedom. He wasn't even thinking about continuing to compete until Jirina Ribbens suggested he contact Roca about the possibility.

SUCCESS AS A COMPETITOR DOES NOT NECESSARILY TRANSLATE TO SUCCESS AS A COACH. THE MOST DECORATED PAIR SKATER IN HISTORY, IRINA RODNINA(LEFT) HAS COACHED ONLY A SINGLE PAIR, CZECHOSLOVAKIA'S KOVARIKOVA AND NOVATNY, TO A WORLD CHAMPIONSHIP, WHILE COUNTRY-WOMAN TAMARA MOSKVINA, WHO, PERSONALLY, WON ONLY A SILVER MEDAL AT THE 1969 WORLDS, HAS COACHED THREE PAIRS TO THE TOP OF THE OLYMPIC PODIUM, AND MANY OTHERS TO NUMEROUS WORLD MEDALS.

The entire Petrenko family moved to the United States together. Along with coach-and-mother-in-law Galina Zmievskaya, Viktor's wife, Nina; brother, Vladimir; and daughter, Viktoria all now make their home in Simsbury, Connecticut.

The case of Oleg Fediukov, who, in 1993, skated at the U.S. Nationals with American Julianna Sachetti, was quite different. The team placed third in the novice division—despite the fact that Oleg had already represented the U.S.S.R. internationally as a senior. The Sachetti family, wanting the best partner they could get for their daughter, traveled to Russia to offer Oleg an all-expense-paid trip to the U.S. (car and green card included). Oleg took the offer, but within a year, he was skating with Laura Gayton—with whom he won the 1994 U.S. junior dance title—as soon as *her* family presented him with a better deal. By 1997, Oleg was skating with his third American partner, Debbie Koegel, whose previous partner, Russian Michael Sklutovsky, won the 1993 U.S. junior dance title with American Kimberly Hartley.

American boys, especially, resented how the Russians had received all their training for free under the old Communist system, and now were cashing in again, as U.S. parents tripped over themselves to become the highest bidder and secure the best boy for their daughter. Even before the rule change to "eligible" and "ineligible," it was hard to consider the newcomers as anything short of professional ringers, even if nothing in the USFSA rulebook prevented non-U.S. citizens from skating at the U.S. Nationals. As skating became increasingly profitable, more and more parents began to see paying for a "professionally" trained partner as the ultimate investment in their daughter's future—no different than buying her the best pair of skates or the prettiest costume in the marketplace.

By the 1996 U.S. Championships, in the senior dance division, seven of the fifteen couples entered featured non-American male partners (five Russian and two British). Both partners of one of the teams, Sophia Eliazova and Peter Tchernyshev, were Russian. They created an added controversy when, instead of following protocol and entering the regional championships, which qualified them for the sectional championships, which qualified them for the Nationals, the team simply dropped into the sectionals, demanding that they be allowed to skate. When they finished third, the referee refused to sign off on the results, claiming they were invalid, and the couple that finished fifth filed a grievance, claiming that, even though they didn't place in the

top four, they should still advance to Nationals, since the number three team was there illegally. In the end, the USFSA, afraid of a full-scale conflict, nullified the sectional results, and granted both teams a bye to the Nationals.

A year later, Peter Tchernyshev was back with a new partner, Naomi Lang. In 1998, when they finished third at the U.S. Nationals, three of the top six teams skating there were non-American (Chalom and British-born Gates placed fourth, and Koegel and Fediukov placed sixth).

Responding to the uproar from U.S. skaters, the USFSA amended its rules to read that non-American citizens could not represent the U.S. at the Olympics or at the World Champion-ships. However, all non-Americans who had already competed at the Nationals prior to the ruling were exempt.

Proponents of foreigners at the U.S. Nationals argue that, in the long run, they will raise the standard of American ice dancing—that if Americans are forced to battle head-to-head with their better-trained international counterparts at the U.S. Nationals, it will inspire them to improve, which will mean a better showing for American teams on the world stage. In the short term, however, a number of U.S. teams have quit skating altogether, frustrated by the knowledge that the opportunity for which they've worked all their lives could be lost to a non-American whose only interest in representing the United States might be a financial one.

An example from the World Championship illustrates the kinds of situations that will arise until the definition of "professional" and the status of foreign skaters fielded by the United States are further clarified. In 1996, American Jenny Dahlen competed in junior dance at the U.S. Nationals with Sergei Lihachov; the team finished seventh. Yet a year later, the girl not good enough to medal at the U.S. Junior Championships was skating at the Worlds with her new partner. Not good enough to beat her fellow Americans, Dahlen had teamed up with a Latvian skater, and went to Worlds representing *his* home country.

THE LONE NON-
RUSSIAN IN THE TOP
THREE AT THE 1999
U.S. DANCE
CHAMPIONSHIP WAS
GREAT BRITAIN'S
MATHEW GATES.
HE AND PARTNER
EVE CHALOM REPRE-
SENTED THE UNITED
STATES AT THE
1999 WORLD
CHAMPIONSHIP, BUT
A FALL IN THE
FREE DANCE LEFT
THEM MIRED IN
SEVENTEENTH PLACE,
AND THEIR FUTURE
STANDING IN THE
AMERICAN ICE
DANCE COMMUNITY
UNCERTAIN.

Off-Ice: Adventures Beyond the Rink

WHERE ONCE AN OLYMPIC MEDAL WAS THE PEAK OF A SKATER'S FAME, CHAMPIONS LIKE CHINA'S LU CHEN(ABOVE) AND THE UNITED STATES' NANCY KERRIGAN(OPPOSITE) NOW HAVE NUMEROUS OPPORTUNITIES TO KEEP THEIR FACES AND NAMES IN THE PUBLIC EYE.

For those few skaters lucky enough to become household names, success on the ice can often translate to opportunities off the ice.

BROADCASTING

The most obvious nonskating venture for many is television commentary. ABC's Dick Button began his broadcast career in 1960, quickly becoming the most controversial personality on the air. No fan lacks an opinion about the gregarious Button—they either love his articulate, suffer-no-fools style or hate his often scathing, finicky critiques. Yet the Harvard graduate, no doubt the most intelligent connoisseur of skating ever to pick up a microphone, defends his manner: "I used to be kinder to skaters years ago. Now, I think this is a major professional activity, and it leads to great amounts of money. I think it's important to be perfectly blunt about what's happening in front of our eyes."

In addition, Carol Heiss Jenkins, Peggy Fleming, John Curry, Scott Hamilton, Rosalynn Sumners, Peter Carruthers, Brian Boitano, Christopher Dean, Christopher Bowman, Kurt Browning, Judy Blumberg, Robin Cousins, Susan Wynne, Midori Ito, Dorothy Hamill, Paul Wylie, Katarina Witt, Ekaterina Gordeeva, Barbara Underhill, Paul Martini, Toller Cranston, Yuka Sato, Daniel Weiss, and Tracy Wilson have all taken a turn behind the microphone. At the 1997 U.S. Championship, Gorsha Sur, though not on camera, helped ABC's Dick Button prepare for and comment on the dance event.

ENDORSEMENTS

Other skaters translate their popularity into a host of endorsements for a variety of skating and non-skating products. Peggy Fleming, Debi Thomas, the Carrutherses, Tara Lipinski, and Todd Eldredge have all hawked Minute Maid. Katarina Witt endorses Swatch, Chen Lu the Omega Watch. Elvis Stojko plugs for Cannon and General Mills, while Bourne and Kraatz appear on a Cheerios box. When Isabelle Duchesnay went to buy a Mazda one day, she was asked to be their official spokesperson in Quebec. Even Brian Boitano's coach, Linda Leaver, secured a spot, pitching prunes on television.

In the winter of 1994, Kristi Yamaguchi starred in a Wendy's hamburger commercial with company chairman Dave Thomas, prompting the U.S. Olympic Committee to accuse the chain of "ambushing" the Winter Olympics' true fast-food sponsor, McDonald's, which had paid close to $40 million for the exclusive right to use Olympic rings in their promotion. The committee claimed Kristi's presence in the ads made it appear that Wendy's was also an official sponsor.

WHEN NICOLE BOBEK, AS ONE OF CAMPBELL SOUP'S SKATING POSTER GIRLS, TRIPPED ALL OVER HERSELF AT THE 1998 OLYMPICS, THE MEDIA JOKED THAT, BACK HOME, STORES WERE REPORTING AN EPIDEMIC OF "SOUP CANS TUMBLING OFF THE SUPERMARKET SHELVES."

Four years later, and just days before the official 1998 U.S. ladies' Olympic team was crowned at the Nationals, Campbell's Soup, a longtime sponsor of key skating tours and shows, made their preferences known to the world when they barraged the airwaves with a commercial featuring Kwan, Lipinski, and Bobek. When that indeed proved to be the U.S. team, ABC commentator Terry Gannon quipped in mock relief, "At least the soup cans are right," prompting mass speculation on the Internet bulletin boards as to whether some kind of corporate-sponsor fix was responsible. Fortunately for Bobek, whose spot on the team was the most precarious, her performance at the Nationals left no doubt that she earned her berth. (One can only wonder what sort of conspiracy rumors might have erupted if results between Bobek and fourth-place finisher Tonia Kwiatkowski had been a closer call.)

When he was still a junior, 1997 and 1998 U.S. silver medalist Michael Weiss starred in a Federal Express commercial as a young skater at the Nationals who is having trouble with his double axel and has to call his grandfather for help. Grandpa dutifully heads to the local rink, where Grandma videotapes him performing the double axel, and off the tape flies to the Nationals, courtesy of FedEx. The ad ran for years. Tai Babilonia and Randy Gardner, 1979 world champions, did a commercial for Nestlé's Crunch, portraying skaters who fall down in competition every time a fan bites her noisy chocolate bar. Despite the falls, Tai and Randy keep smiling with delight, prompting the judges to reward them numerous 10s.

Scott Williams, 1987 U.S. bronze medalist, appeared in probably the most recognized skating commercial, though his face was never seen. In 1996, Scott was the body double for Dunkin' Donuts' Fred the Baker as he jumped and spun on the ice while clutching a coffeepot. A year later, Scott's wife, Canadian champion Charlene Wong, twirled on TV for a skating Barbie ad, with the doll's image later superimposed over hers. Following the 1998 Olympics, it was Tara Lipinski's turn to twirl alongside Barbie, though *her* image was quite visible.

In 1995, as the entire skating world shuddered through its pro evolution, Finnish ice dancers and 1995 world silver medalists Susanna Rahkamo and Petri Kokko became the first to take advertising to the next level when, at the Europeans and the Worlds, Kokko's costume bore, tennis-style, their sponsor's logo (Nokkia). At the 1998 Olympics, as Germans Wotzel and Steuer practiced dressed in black outfits with large white swans drawn on the back, onlookers wondered whether the lovely birds had to do with the theme of their program. The answer was no: it was the theme of their sponsor.

ACTING

Aside from appearing in various forms of advertising, a few skaters possess faces famous enough to earn them guest spots on some of television's favorite shows. Peggy Fleming popped up on *Newhart*, where she reminded Tom Poston, "It's never too late to learn to swim," and on *Diagnosis: Murder*, where the guilty party was revealed when sleuth Dick Van Dyke, by looking at blade marks on the ice, deduced that only the blonde skater with a triple axel in her arsenal could have left those scratches. Not even Fleming could get to Dick in time to explain that all axels, single, double, or triple, leave the same scrapes, and there's no way to guess by looking at them how many revolutions were actually performed in the air.

Dorothy Hamill appeared on *Diff'rent Strokes*, Tara Lipinski on *Early Edition*, and Nancy Kerrigan on *Boy Meets World* and *Saturday Night Live*, where she skated a duet with the late Chris Farley. (*Saturday Night Live* has a tradition of mocking skaters, as the show often airs immediately after the men's long program at the Olympics. In 1988, Tom Hanks played "Mark Massano," who wore a tight

bodysuit and cowboy hat and commiserated over his "0.0" scores with Dick Button [Phil Hartman] and Peggy Fleming [Nora Dunn]. In 1992, Jason Priestley wiped up the ice while Scott Hamilton [Dana Carvey] could only "ooh" and "ow" after every painful fall. In 1998, Sarah Michelle Gellar played a chain-smoking Tara Lipinski.)

The most prolific actress has been Katarina Witt. Through her own company, With Witt, she produced a very successful film in Germany, *Ice Princess*, which costarred Rosalynn Sumners and Toller Cranston. In America, Katarina has appeared in commercials for Diet Coke, played herself on TV in *Arli$$* and *Everybody Loves Raymond*, and appeared in the blockbuster film *Jerry Maguire*,

THE MOST RECOGNIZABLE FIGURE-SKATING COVERAGE TEAM IN THE WORLD: ABC'S DICK BUTTON AND PEGGY FLEMING. IN 1996, BRIAN BOITANO JOINED THE BROADCASTING CREW TO HELP DICK WITH THE MEN'S COMPETITION AT NATIONALS AND WORLDS.

where, Katarina enthused, "I got to hug Tom Cruise!"

Fellow 1994 Olympian Tonya Harding costarred with somewhat lesser names when she appeared in *Breakaway*, a 35mm production with a budget of $70,000 and no distributor; she played a raunchy waitress who gets mixed up in mob business. In the meantime, Nancy Kerrigan, who whether she likes it or not will always be linked in the public's mind with her ex-

teammate, starred in the video series *Fairy Tales on Ice* as Alice in Wonderland.

Hoping for a career on the big screen once her time on the ice is up, two-time Olympic dance champion Pasha Grishuk had a meeting with director John Frankenheimer, who offered her a role in his film *Ronin*. Grishuk could not accept the part because filming would have conflicted with her training for the 1998 Olympics. The role went instead to the ever-popular Witt. When Grishuk bad-mouthed her replacement to the press, Frankenheimer sent a letter to the *Herald-Tribune*, asserting, "The luckiest thing that happened to me in filming *Ronin* was that Miss Grishuk was unavailable. Miss Witt brought a lovely quality of vulnerability and beauty to the role, which I do not feel Miss Grishuk ever could have done."

While the women of skating prefer to grace the big and little screens, the men tend to gravitate toward the theater. Dick Button, after a brief stint

performing on the stage, including as the juvenile lead in *Call Me Madam*, progressed to producing plays like Tom Stoppard's *Artist Descending a Staircase* and *Sweet Sue*, with Mary Tyler Moore and Lynn Redgrave. John Curry appeared in *Twelfth Night* and *She Stoops to Conquer* in England, *Brigadoon* on Broadway, and *Privates on Parade* at New York's Roundabout Theater. Curry's countryman Robin Cousins donned a fur bodysuit to portray Munkustrap in *Cats* and fishnet stockings for his role as Dr. Frank-N-Furter in *The Rocky Horror Picture Show*. Cousins can also be heard on the CDs *Joseph and the Amazing Technicolor Dreamcoat* and *Songs of Andrew Lloyd Webber*, and seen (though not heard) in a small role in the theatrical film *The Cutting Edge*. He choreographed all the skating sequences for the movie, casting many American and Canadian skaters in bit parts, and personally played the character of a television commentator—only to find himself dubbed over when the producers decided his British accent didn't fit the sound they were looking for.

Yet another British skater, Christopher Dean, choreographed an autobiographical ballet for the English National Ballet in Cambridge. Set to six songs by Paul Simon, *Encounters* told the story of Dean's life as defined by five key women: his mother, his stepmother, his partner, Jayne Torvill, and his two wives (former pupil Isabelle Duchesnay and 1990 world champion Jill Trenary).

NANCY KERRIGAN'S POST-OLYMPIC RELATIONSHIP WITH DISNEY WENT SOUR AFTER SHE ALLEGEDLY ACCUSED MICKEY MOUSE OF BEING "CORNY." FORTUNATELY, AMERICA'S 1998 MEDALISTS HAD A WARMER RELATIONSHIP WITH THE MOUSE. TARA LIPINSKI SPENT ALL OF HER SUMMER VACATIONS AT DISNEY WORLD IN FLORIDA, AND MADE HER SECRET WISH FOR OLYMPIC GOLD SITTING IN FRONT OF SNOW WHITE'S CASTLE, WHILE MICHELLE KWAN SIGNED A DEAL TO STAR IN A SERIES OF DISNEY TELEVISION SPECIALS.

BOOKS

With the ever-growing popularity of skating, the demand for skaters and skating-related books have reached an all-time high, prompting many a medalist to turn author. In the years surrounding the 1998 Olympics, Elvis Stojko, Tara Lipinski, Rudy Galindo, Torvill and Dean, Toller Cranston, Sandra Bezic, Ekaterina Gordeeva, Brasseur and Eisler, the Duchesnays, Kristi Yamaguchi, and Oksana Baiul have all released autobiographies. Biographies of Scott Hamilton, Robin Cousins, Michelle Kwan, 01and Tara Lipinski have also hit the shelves. Brian Boitano penned a combination autobiography and skating history, while Kristi Yamaguchi put her name on *Skating for Dummies*. Before any medals were even awarded in Japan, 1998 U.S. champion Michelle Kwan had a deal with Scholastic Books for an autobiography, a poster book, and a scrapbook with a reproduction of the dragon pendant she wears around her neck for luck.

Then there are those skaters whose off-ice endeavors, courtesy of the fame they achieved while on it, can be classified only under the ubiquitous category: "Other."

OTHER VENTURES

Denise Biellmann, 1981 world champion, not satisfied with hitting her stride in professional skating competitions, also wants to be the Jane Fonda of Europe. She has developed a fitness machine, health foods, and a clothing line currently being sold exclusively through a boutique in Zurich. Denise told *International Figure Skating*, "I don't want to sell [my products] as the ice-skater. I want to get into the market as Denise Biellmann, the fashion designer....Of course, my name helps."

Meanwhile, a short plane flight away, 1997 world pair champion Ingo Steuer is capitalizing on his famous name to open, in his hometown of Chemnitz, Germany, Ingo's WashPub, a unique establishment where customers can do their laundry and have a beer at the same time.

IN 1998, WORLD PAIR CHAMPION ISABELLE BRASSEUR (LEFT, WITH PARTNER LLOYD EISLER) REVEALED THAT SHE WAS SUFFERING FROM A HEART CONDITION THAT CAUSED HER TO EXPERIENCE SEIZURES, THUS PUTTING HER FUTURE SKATING CAREER IN JEOPARDY.

OFF-ICE: ADVENTURES BEYOND THE RINK

In America, skaters Rocky Marval and Alexander Zhulin became not only clients of Marco Entertainment, a management and promotion company, but also its two newest vice presidents. Nicole Bobek got to step into an unfamiliar arena and live out her lifelong dream by posing for a *Vogue* layout entitled "Wild in Winter." And for those winter Olympians curious to see how the other half lives, Kristi Yamaguchi, Peggy Fleming, Nancy Kerrigan, Peter Oppegard, Elizabeth Punsalan, and Kitty Carruthers were able to do their part for the 1996 Summer Olympics as torch-bearing runners for the countrywide journey to Atlanta.

CHARITY WORK

Along with the professional and personal perks that accompany being a worldwide star come responsibilities. Most skaters take these responsibilities very seriously, using their celebrity status to support a multitude of favorite charities and causes.

Scott Hamilton donates $2 from every *Stars on Ice* ticket purchased with a Discover Card to the local Make-a-Wish Foundation. Kristi Yamaguchi, with support from Paul Wylie, Peggy Fleming, Chen Lu, and Rosalynn Sumners, sponsors an in-line Skate-a-Thon in San Francisco's Golden Gate Park to raise money for her personal Always Dream Foundation, whose beneficiaries include the Japanese-American Children's Cultural and Arts Fund. Debi Thomas finds time around her time-consuming medical school schedule to speak at Soar for Success, a program directed at motivating young women to pursue traditionally male careers. Kurt Browning serves as ambassador for the Muscular Dystrophy Association of Canada, while his association with sponsor Kellogg's led to the creation of the Browning Fund, which supports young Canadian skaters. For the 1997–1998 season, Cook's Champagne, the primary sponsor of Todd Eldredge, pledged to donate $1,000 to City of Hope, a medical research center, every time Todd lands a triple jump in competition through the 1998 Nationals.

Tragically, the cause many skaters find themselves closest to is AIDS research. So many skaters and

ALONG WITH HER MONETARY CHILDREN'S CHARITY, OLYMPIC CHAMPION KRISTI YAMAGUCHI TAKES THE HANDS-ON APPROACH TO HER GOOD DEEDS, HELPING YOUNGSTERS WITH DISABILITIES GET A "LEG UP" ON THE ICE.

those around the sport have died from the disease that Brian Orser, after losing his friend, 1988 Olympic dance bronze medalist Rob McCall, in 1992, spearheaded *Skate the Dream*, an on-ice tribute to all those who have passed away. The spark for the Rob McCall Centre for HIV Research fund-raiser came from Rob himself, who, in the days before he died, worked to make the show happen. The title referred to Rob's dream of coming up with a cure and of seeing his favorite skaters performing together. CTV aired the special across Canada and solicited donations from viewers. Not only did Orser produce the subsequent *Skate the Dream*, he also, through his Brian Orser Productions, developed several benefits for the Calgary Hospital and became the national spokesperson for Friends with AIDS.

Because of their contributions to so many grand-scale worthy causes, it would seem the busy skaters wouldn't have time to take an interest in individu-als. Yet ABC's Doug Wilson reveals that the opposite is true. He explains, "When my wife died, I thought that [to the skaters] I was just the TV guy who showed up now and then at an event. My wife had requested that a fund be started to renovate the sac-risty in our church. I didn't even reach out and let anybody in the skating world know about this. The day after she died, a phone call came from Tom Collins. Another phone call came from Jill Trenary. The first significant check for the renovation of the sacristy arrived from Scott Hamilton. In 1991, I found out the skating world has a huge heart."

FOLLOWING THE DEATH OF HIS CLOSE FRIEND ROB MCCALL, BRIAN ORSER SKATED THE EMOTIONAL "MY BUDDY" IN HIS HONOR. ALTHOUGH SEVERAL TOP SKATERS HAVE LOST THEIR LIVES TO AIDS—INCLUDING 1976 OLYMPIC CHAMPION JOHN CURRY—THE SPORT'S GOVERNING BODIES HAVE DONE LITTLE TO EDUCATE THEIR ATHLETES ABOUT THE DISEASE.

SKATING'S FUTURE

WHILE ONCE ONLY AN OLYMPIC GOLD MEDALIST COULD HAVE CONFIDENTLY EXPECTED TO EARN AMPLE
MONEY FOR PERFORMING, THESE DAYS, A SKATER LIKE DAN HOLLANDER (ABOVE), WHO FAILED TO SO MUCH
AS QUALIFY FOR AN OLYMPIC TEAM, CAN MAKE A LIVING SKATING. AND FOR YOUNGSTERS LIKE 1999 U.S.
SILVER MEDALIST NAOMI NARI NAM (OPPOSITE), THE FUTURE APPEARS LIMITLESS.

While Olympic medalists from Peggy Fleming to Kristi Yamaguchi did profit from the competitive and exhibition opportunities of the skating-mad 1990s, the group that benefited most from the sport's professional explosion was the colloquially dubbed "middle class" of skaters. These were the skaters who never won Olympic gold or a medal of any kind on the world level, and once might have believed their careers were over. Asserts Meg Streeter, "The greatest thing [skating's recent popularity] did was give many skaters a chance to have a life after eligible skating. There's a whole middle level now. They love to skate, and they've been able to continue their careers."

NEW OPPORTUNITIES FOR SECOND-TIER SKATERS

Athletes who might have stopped skating because there was no place for them in the narrow professional world are continuing to compete, and in some cases are performing better than they did as amateurs. Denise Biellmann is one such skater. Caryn Kadavy is another. The 1987 world bronze medalist had to withdraw from the 1988 Olympics because she had the flu, and she won no major amateur titles. Yet she flourished as a professional, winning the 1993 U.S. Open, Miko Masters, and Hershey's Kisses Pro/Am. In the Pro/Am, Caryn defeated then–U.S. champion Nancy Kerrigan as well as 1990 world champion Jill Trenary. Caryn gushed, "This has really enhanced my career. It's something I never thought could happen. This was like the Olympics I never had."

Jirina Ribbens believes that "Caryn is better now than she was as an amateur because she got over the jitters. She is now a good competitor, whereas before she didn't have that mental strength."

Another skater whose amateur career was plagued by nerves is the Russian pair skater Elena Bechke. She and then-husband Denis Petrov finished second at the 1992 Olympics, but could do no better than a bronze at the 1989 Worlds, mostly because of Elena's tendency to fall apart under pressure. Yet becoming a pro and skating every night with Stars on Ice, as well as coming out to do an occasional competition once in a while, taught her that nothing was do or die. Elena learned that she could win one day and lose the next, and the world would keep turning. As a result, she gained control over her nerves and was rewarded with four consecutive second places at the World Pro, followed by a triumphant win in 1996.

Czechoslovakia's Jozef Sabovcik retired from the amateur world with a best of third at the 1984 Olympics. With no other titles, and coming from

a then-Communist country, his prospects looked even more dismal than Bechke and Petrov's. Yet a move West allowed Jozef to break through the "invitation-only" glass ceiling of professional competitions. Unlike Scott Hamilton and Brian Orser, with whom he shared an Olympic podium, Jozef did not start at the top. He never received an invitation to World Pro. When he won the World Cup of Skating in 1990, fans began taking notice of the only pro on the circuit to boast a triple axel, a backflip, and a quadruple toe loop. As word about "Jumpin' Joe" grew, so did the offers coming his way. He finished second at the 1995 Miko Masters, won the 1996 Rowenta Masters, placed second at the 1996 Canadian Pro and Challenge of Champions, and, in 1997, took part in Battle of the Sexes, Ice Wars, World Team, and Legends. But perhaps nothing else speaks to Jozef's popularity among skating fans more than the sight of teddy bears scattered on the ice after his performances, designated gifts for Jozef's toddler son, Blade.

The need to fill slotsint the seemingly never-ending number of pro competitions on the calendar also proved a godsend for a pair of truly international teams. American Renee Roca and Russian-born Gorsha Sur had skated seriously together for only six weeks when they made their competitive debut at the 1990 World Pro. Everything happened so quickly that Renee had to buy the burgundy dress she wore for the technical program off the rack and hastily decree it a skating outfit. They took a quick detour into the reinstated amateur ranks, winning the U.S. dance titles in 1993 and 1995. In 1996, they turned pro for a second time, finishing third at the 1996 World Pro. Muses Jirina Ribbens, "They had to get back into the groove, become better performers again, focus less on technical skills." A year later, the couple did just that, winning the 1997 World Pro over Usova and Zhulin, a team who, in 1993, were crowned world champions while Renee and Gorsha placed eleventh.

Unlike Roca and Sur, the Russian/American pairing of Mishkutenok and Shepherd has yet to win

any pro titles, but the fact that they are even competing at all is a testament to the opportunities now available to skaters without world or Olympic medals, or, in this case, to a team where only one of the partners has those credentials.

Russia's Natalia Mishkutenok retired from amateur skating in 1994 after winning the Olympic pair gold in 1992 and the Olympic pair silver in 1994 with partner Artur Dmitriev. Then, in November of 1994, Natalia ran into American hockey player Craig Shepherd in Moscow while he was making a stammering attempt, in Russian, to buy a cup of orange juice. Natalia came to Craig's rescue. He bought his juice. They never saw each other again for the duration of Craig's Russian stay. A year later, it was Natalia's turn to visit the United States—Colorado Springs to be precise—where friends recommended she consult with their new local strength and conditioning coach. When Craig arrived to pick Natalia up at her house, he told *International Figure Skating*, "She didn't know it was going to be me. We thought we had lost each other. It was like *Dr. Zhivago*."

The couple married in July 1996 and, inspired by the film *The Cutting Edge*, soon decided to form a pair on the ice as well as off. Thanks to Natalia's extensive pair experience, lifts were no problem. Even the throws, which can be cheated if the woman knows what she's doing, eventually came

along. But as a hockey player, Craig never had a reason to jump or spin—a visible deficiency in a figure skater. Nevertheless, by 1997, the brand-new team had not only an agent but an invitation to perform in a prestigious exhibition, *Evening with Champions*, and compete at the U.S. Open.

None of the "middle-class" skaters named above would have been able to keep honing their technical and artistic skills had it not been for the surge of curiosity about skating. But the current plethora of competitions still isn't enough for 1986 U.S. silver

medalist Scott Williams. A two-time world competitor, Williams, according to Meg Streeter, "is committed to giving skaters who may not be Olympic gold medalists, or have the big professional titles, a chance to show what they can do and shine."

To that end Williams, with his wife, Charlene Wong, produced the first American Open Professional Figure Skating Championship in May 1997. Though the event failed to break even financially, it did grant the opportunity for a number of skaters not fortunate enough to find themselves on the A or even the B list of invitational professional events to compete and perform. Said Williams to *International Figure Skating*, "Our goal was to make sure our skaters had a chance to meet, get seen, and hear comments from people in the industry that hire and are involved in the production, choreography and direction of various ice shows."

SCOTT WILLIAMS' PROFESSIONAL COMPETITIONS FOR SKATERS UNABLE TO EARN AN INVITATION TO THE MORE PRESTIGIOUS EVENTS HAS OPENED THE DOOR FOR NUMEROUS UNKNOWN TALENTS. TO SUPPORT SCOTT'S EFFORTS, BRIAN BOITANO INVITED THE WINNERS FROM SCOTT'S AMERICAN OPEN TO PERFORM IN HIS TELEVISION SPECIAL, SKATE AGAINST HATE.

Another open competition premiering in 1997 was the U.S. Open Professional Championship. The winners of the pair event, Russians Elena Leonova and Andrei Khvalko—a tandem that began skating together only in 1995 and could claim neither amateur nor profes- sional titles—made such an impression that they received an invitation to compete at the 1997 World Pro.

Such ascension to more prestigious events is precisely what the producers of the open competitions had in mind when arranging their events. It is also what many skating insiders would like to see as the next logical step in their sport— the establishment of a pro qualifying circuit.

Streeter explains, "I have never once been on the edge of my seat at a professional competition, because they're invitational. Nobody qualifies. There hasn't been a whole series of qualifying rounds to get there. Sure it's interesting to see if Brian Boitano is going to beat Kurt Browning. But it's not the same as a warmup at the [eligible] World Championships where four or five men could win the event, and they all had to qualify to get there....[In the Pros] there's no circuit, there's no buildup to a final, supreme night."

ABC's Doug Wilson concurs: "I would love to see it have some kind of form. So that people could plan to look at it, and anticipate the professional championships."

Streeter, however, doesn't think that's likely to happen soon, because "that would require all the people who run the professional events to work together and put together a circuit that's fair and works towards one main [competition]. It would mean putting aside self-interest for the larger inter- est of an international professional championship, one that has skaters from all over the world com- peting for the top title that really means something.

I just would like to see the pro circuit generate as much anticipation and excitement about who the winner is going to be as in the eligible ranks."

In their crusade to generate such excitement, Candid Productions is working on

creating that structured pro circuit. Already, winners of the U.S. Pro and Challenge of Champions are guaranteed an invitation to the World Pro, and by 2000, the company hopes to broadcast their compe- tition live, in late January, so that it might truly be the culminating event of the pro season.

Wilson summarizes, "Pro events are fun events. I think boys against girls are fun. I think Pro/Ams are fun. I think the big-money events, [like] Ice Wars, are fun. I think they have their place. But I would like to see the nurturing of the high quality skater. I would like to see the level of excellence continue to grow. Not only along the gymnastic side of skat- ing, but in the artistic side. I want to be sure skating holds on to the artistry, and that the artistic side of skating is maintained as the backdrop against which the tricks are done."

For those performers whose version of a skating utopia agrees with Wilson's, the fastest growing outlet for their talent is the proliferation of new ice theaters across the country. Strictly noncompetitive and structured like traditional dance companies, ice theaters are another venue offering the "middle-class" skater a forum for his or her talents.

The City of Angels Ice Theater, dedicated to the development of skating as a theatrical art form, was established in Los Angeles when various skating professionals, including Lisa-Marie Allen, Jim Yorke, and Bobby Beauchamp—the first African-American to participate in an international competition, the 1979 World Junior Championship—began meeting for a weekly on-ice exercise class. They made their debut in 1995 at an AIDS benefit in Las Vegas. Colorado's Ice West Contemporary Ice Theater was founded by Tom Dickson and his wife, Catarina Lindgren, who want to bring a "contemporary edge" to their ice theater, while the Seattle Ice Theater's Becci Safai hopes her troupe will prove that Olympic champion credentials aren't indispensable to a skating company's success.

While ice theaters have yet to establish themselves as firmly in the commercial marketplace as tours and competitions, they are starting to receive critical recognition. Maryland's Next Ice Age artistic director, Nathan Birch, is the only skating choreographer ever to be awarded a grant from the National Endowment for the Arts, while the Ice Theatre of New York is the only skating company to receive organizational funding from the same source.

According to Streeter, the range of choices available, from competitions to tours to ice theaters, "bodes well for our eligible skaters because [before], you knew if you didn't make it, if you didn't become Dorothy Hamill, you didn't have any choices. Now, young skaters can see that if they don't win a big title, but if they really love to skate, there are places where they can skate and make a decent living."

CROWD-PLEASERS

Taking into account the wealth of opportunities beckoning from every direction, the future of those skaters giving up their eligible status following the 1998 Olympics—both the ones who medaled and the ones who didn't—can easily be considered brighter than any previous generation's. Even those who failed to make the Olympic team are facing choices that were unimaginable only a few years earlier.

Dan Hollander's inability to qualify for the final round at the 1997 World Championship meant that the United States would be allowed to send only two men to the Olympics. Popular wisdom in skating ran that, as a two-time U.S. bronze medalist, the

Olympic spot that Dan lost was his own. Some expected him to quit. But Dan decided to make one more run at the Olympics. He fired his longtime coach, Diana Ronayne, by letter, an approach that devastated her with its cold impersonality, and moved to a new training base. His last-ditch attempt did Dan little good, however. At the 1998 Nationals, he finished in sixth place.

The 1998 U.S. bronze went to Scott Davis, another skater who, two years earlier, had left his longtime coach, Kathy Casey, to train with Galina Zmievskaya, coach of Viktor Petrenko and Oksana Baiul. Scott's third-place finish was a vindication of sorts, as it was his first time back on the medal podium after winning back-to-back U.S. titles in 1993 and 1994 and finishing second in 1995 before dropping to fourth in 1996 and 1997. In many other years, third place would have earned him a trip to the Olympics or Worlds. But in 1998, it only marked Scott's final eligible competition.

The future still holds ample professional possibilities for Scott and Dan. Both are audience-pleasing entertainers—Dan's mime routine and Scott's Zorba the Greek are showstoppers even without jumps—who could tour with Disney-type shows. While an invitation to the World Professional Championship or Challenge of Champions is unlikely, either skater could be a record-setting champion on the type of circuit set up by Scott Williams. They could also follow the example of Aren Nielsen. A U.S. bronze medalist in 1994 and 1995, Aren never earned a U.S. title or a world or Olympic

medal. He also tried a last-ditch coaching change, leaving Carol Heiss Jenkins for Don Laws, only to place a devastating eighth at the Nationals in 1996 and ninth in 1997. Yet even before leaving the eligible ranks, Aren was able to perform with professionals like Brian Boitano and Caryn Kadavy in *Skating Romance*. This opportunity provided him with an exemplary transition as, without missing a beat, Aren returned to *Skating Romance III* after officially turning pro.

Another skater who failed to make his Olympic team, Russia's Alexei Urmanov, is in a different situation from Hollander, Davis, and Nielson, in that Alexei was already the men's Olympic gold medalist

in 1994. Rather than immediately turning pro, Alexei elected to remain eligible, as both he and his coach, Alexei Mishin, felt that an Olympic victory without a world title to back it up was a hollow one. In the years between Olympics, Alexei failed to win the world title he so craved, though he came the closest in 1997 in Switzerland. After winning his qualifying round with a flawless long program and then placing first in the short program, Alexei was forced to withdraw from the competition because of a groin injury, the irony being that he'd already skated a short and long program worthy of a gold medal—only in the wrong order! That groin injury, among others, kept him from defending his Olympic title in Nagano. Mishin insisted that Alexei remain eligible for one more year—they still wanted that crack at a world title. Many wondered

if that was really the best course of action under the circumstances. As things stood, Alexei already boasted the distinction of being "the forgotten Olympic champion." Because he didn't turn pro right after his victory and didn't cash in immediately, his name recognition, especially among North American fans—the ones who spend 80 percent of the money raked in by skating shows, tours, and pro competitions—was minimal. His disappearance from the 1997–1998 competitive scene, which allowed another Russian, Ilia Kulik, to win both the Olympic gold and the hordes of screaming teenage girls, only made matters worse. Unlike Petrenko, Boitano, Hamilton, and Cousins, Alexei Urmanov may sadly discover that his golden chance on the pro circuit came and went while he was busy chasing a dream.

For those skaters whose dreams culminated only in making their respective Olympic teams, those for whom a medal was always a long shot, the professional opportunities are also plentiful. For the husband-and-wife teams of pair skaters Jenni Meno and Todd Sand and dancers Elizabeth Punsalan and Jerod Swallow, their popularity with North American audiences guarantees invitations to pro competitions where they can go head-to-head against world champions like Wotzel and Steuer or Grishuk and Platov—only this time, like Roca and Sur's upset victory over Usova and Zhulin at the 1997 World Pro, with better results.

The Americans' future looks even brighter than that of Russia's 1996 world champions Eltsova and Bushkov. One of the most uncharismatic pairs ever to stand on the podium, their failure to win a medal in Nagano may very well have cost them a professional career. After weighing their options, the team split up in May of 1998. Agent Michael Rosenberg

plary routine complete with a quadruple toe loop—the jump that Todd tried, and fell on, at the Nationals. The sight of Ilia Kulik's perfection and resulting the scores visibly rattled Todd, and when he stepped onto the ice, it was tentatively, his eyes darting nervously from side to side. As the mistakes piled up in his long program and the music drummed toward its end, Todd tried to squeak out a second, unplanned triple axel, crashing to the ground in a culmination of the year's anxiety.

Todd finished the 1998 Olympics in fourth place, as did Russia's Maria Butyrskaya, a skater whose professional future is up in the air. Unlike Todd, Maria's presentation has always been the strongest part of her routines, earning comparisons to Madonna for her vogue style of vamping. But competition for places on the professional circuit is brutal. Even a well-liked world champion like Yuka Sato failed to earn an invitation to the 1997 World Pro because the powers that be concluded she hadn't skated well enough technically during the course of the season. Maria, a skater whose jumps tend to desert her at the first sign of nerves, is neither a big enough name (like Olympic champion Oksana Baiul) to make up for that deficiency with crowd appeal nor consistent enough (like Denise Biellmann) to make up for the lack of name recognition with technically dazzling programs. However, if she, like Caryn Kadavy and Elena Bechke, could conquer her stage fright, her all-important showmanship could give Maria the edge in the professional word.

The fourth-place finishers in ice dance, Canada's Shae-Lynn Bourne and Victor Kraatz, are likely to do just as well professionally without an Olympic medal as they would have done with

of Marco Entertainment explains that, to be successful on the pro circuit, a skater must have showmanship. According to him, that's why 1994 and 1998 Olympic bronze medalist Philippe Candeloro will be a "multimillionaire" while 1994 Olympic gold medalist Alexei Urmanov "makes zippo." Eltsova and Bushkov have no showmanship.

Neither does five-time U.S. champion Todd Eldredge, who, like Eltsova and Bushkov, came to the Olympics with a 1996 world title to his credit and left without a medal. Todd's final eligible season seemed to be drenched in sweaty, teeth-clenching desperation, a sense of "This is it. Now or never. Do or die." Responding to printed accusations that his presentation lacked...presentation, Todd changed his short program in the month between the Nationals and the Olympics. Then, at the Games, Todd made the mistake of standing at the barrier and watching eventual winner Kulik skate an exem-

THOUGH HE
PUBLICLY DECLINED
TO PARTICIPATE IN
THE 1998– 1999
ELIGIBLE SEASON,
TODD ELDREDGE IS
KEEPING HIS OPTIONS
OPEN, AND NOT
WHOLLY DISCOUNT-
ING A RETURN TRIP
TO THE OLYMPICS IN
2002.

one. Immensely popular in their home country, Shae-Lynn and Victor have already appeared in the *Elvis Tour* and on several television specials. In fact, the oft-repeated contention that they were "robbed" of a medal in Nagano will probably only add to their marketability.

The two skaters with the most uncertain future ahead of them are also two of the sport's most eccentric characters. France's Surya Bonaly finished tenth at the 1998 Olympics, while the United States' Nicole Bobek ended up seventeenth. Both have a tendency to rechoreograph their programs in the middle of a performance, switch compulsively from coach to coach in the hope of finding a magic formula, and give up during a competition if the tide doesn't appear to be flowing their way. In addition, as her parting shot at a judging establishment she always contended was against her, Surya, in the middle of her long program at the 1998 Olympics, deliberately executed her trademark backflip—an illegal maneuver in eligible competition.

Despite their respective problems and reputations, neither Surya nor Nicole have ever lacked crowd-pleasing charisma. Both were huge hits with *Champions on Ice,* and are well known enough in America and Europe to draw audiences eager to find out just what these "bad girls of skating" might do next. Agent Michael Rosenberg believes that Surya has the potential to earn up to $1 million as a professional.

This is a healthy sum by most people's estimates, but not even close to the "five or ten million" Rosenberg thinks Michelle Kwan should be able to earn even without an Olympic gold medal. Apparently, grace in defeat has become such a rare commodity in America that when Michelle didn't respond to her second-place finish by hurling chairs through a window or whining to the press and bad-mouthing her opponent, it was enough to prompt a media frenzy lauding her unusually good sportsmanship, followed by a host of endorsement and television special offers. Michelle's public persona, already pristine, was boosted further by her graciousness in Nagano and earned the teenager even more fans.

Unfortunately, despite her swelling popularity, Michelle did not have the option of turning pro to take advantage of her status following the 1998 World Championships. She had already signed a contract with Turner Television to compete in their 1998 Goodwill Games, and so had to hold onto her eligible status at least until the summer. Of course, immediately after the Olympics, Michelle swore she had every intention of staying eligible for another four years so that she could, once again, go for the gold in Salt Lake City in 2002. However, many questioned the wisdom of this. It would be almost unprecedented for a skater to maintain her level of excellence for such a long time, though Katarina Witt did pull off the feat in 1984 and 1988. Unlike Michelle, however, Witt had not won a world title two years earlier. Happy though she was when Michelle won the Worlds in 1996, Peggy Fleming worried that it was too early for her to peak, and predicted Michelle would have a tough time keeping her momentum going until the 1998 Olympics. It seems unlikely that she could last until the 2002 Olympics.

In addition, there is also the Urmanov factor. By not cashing in at the height of her medal-drenched popularity, Kwan risks being eclipsed by a perkier, younger, up-and-coming skater and missing her window of peak professional opportunity.

One athlete with no intention of letting his opportunity pass by is France's Philippe Candeloro. Shrewdly aware that a repeat of his come-from-behind bronze medal triumph at the 1998 Olympics was unlikely, Philippe announced his probable retirement from eligible skating at the post-Olympic press conference, as well as plans for touring with *Champions on Ice* and a European tour of his own.

That tour would probably be similar to that of Elvis Stojko, who struggled with a groin injury at the Olympics but whose silver medal there in no way took the luster off his popularity in Canada and elsewhere. In fact, considering that Elvis already had all those things you once needed a gold medal to get—a tour, endorsements, invitations to professional competitions—it could be postulated that a win at the Olympics would have been...nice, but hardly the career maker it would have been in the past.

If Elvis demonstrated one principle with his eligible activities, it was that the idea of an Olympic medal as the key to the future is virtually obsolete. The new pros are those skaters, eligible and ineligible, who regardless of titles can fill coliseums with fans and promote TV ratings. Instant fame at the Olympics is now merely one of many ways to achieve that level of name recognition. There are also professional competitions, made-for-TV specials, touring companies, and ice theaters.

Now that figure skating has finally become a thriving professional endeavor, the avenues to success in the sport are as diverse as the personalities who grace it.

1999 U.S. BRONZE
MEDALIST TIMOTHY
GOEBEL MADE HIS-
TORY AT THE 1999
WORLD
CHAMPIONSHIPS
WHEN HE LANDED AN
UNPRECEDENTED
QUADRUPLE SAL-
CHOW/TRIPLE TOE
LOOP COMBINATION
IN THE QUALIFYING
ROUND, AND THEN,
AGAIN, DURING HIS
LONG PROGRAM.

INDEX

PHOTO CREDITS